CAVALRY BITS
One of Seven Volumes

The Yellowstone Expedition of 1873

Custer on hunt along Yellowstone in 1873.

CAVALRY BITS
One of Seven Volumes

The Yellowstone Expedition of 1873

JOHN M. CARROLL, General Editor
William Gardner Bell, Introduction to Series
Dr. Lawrence A. Frost, Afterword
Don Trioni and Scott Myers, Illustrators

J. M. CARROLL & COMPANY
Mattituck and Bryan

Copyright © 1986
J. M. Carroll & Company
Mattituck, New York and Bryan, Texas
All rights reserved

Articles Originally Appearing in
Cavalry Journal

International Standard Book Number 0-8844-0205-5 (volume)
International Standard Book Number 0-8844-0040-0 (set)

To order contact
J. M. Carroll & Company
Post Office Box 1200
Mattituck, New York 11952

Manufactured in the United States by The Mad Printers of Mattituck

For Command Sergeant Major Douglas Hayes of the 1st Cavalry Division at Fort Hood, Texas. In Recognition Of His Thirty Years In The U. S. Army And Especially For His Last Fifteen Years In The Cavalry. A True Son Of The Yellow.

FIRST TEAM! GARRY OWEN!

Table of Contents

Introduction to the Series 9
Foreword 25
The Yellowstone Expedition of 1873 43
An Incident of the Yellowstone Expedition
    of 1873 85
Afterword 101
Appendix 109
Pywell's Photographs 115
Index 165

Brigadier General David S. Stanley, Commander of Yellowstone Expedition of 1873. From the John M. Carroll Collection.

Theodore W. Goldin, Janesville, Mississippi. Troop "G" 7th USC, Xmas 1895. So often cited in this book, particularly his letters to and from Capt. Benteen. From the John M. Carroll Collection.

1st Lt. Edward S. Godfrey at the time of the Yellowstone Expedition of 1873. From the U. S. Army Military History Institute.

Rain-in-the-Face, who boasted of killing the sutler and veterinarian and soldier on the Yellowstone Expedition of 1873. From the John M. Carroll Collection.

Frederick Benteen, so often cited in footnotes in this book. From the John M. Carroll Collection.

Frederick Benteen after retirement and brevetted Brigadier General. From the U. S. Army Military History Institute.

Cadet Braden. Taken in 1869 at West Point just prior to graduation in 1869. From the John M. Carroll Collection.

Lt. Charles Braden, 7th Cavalry. Braden was stationed in New Orleans from 3 December 1872 through 31 March 1873. This picture was taken there. From the U. S. Army Military History Institute.

Introduction to Series

The period from 1881 up to the Spanish American War has been called the United States Army's Renaissance. In that span of years the foundations of American military professionalism were laid down. This was no precise and planned development, but a groping evolution that materialized from and overcame what has been called the Army's Dark Ages — the period from the Civil War up to 1880, when declining strength, inadequate appropriations and pay, inefficient organization, wide dispersion, a provincial existence, and a hostile society, all combined to reduce the Army to such a low estate that a rising sentiment for reform and position was inevitable. It was a sign of the times when, on November 9, 1885, a group of cavalry officers at Fort Leavenworth met to form the U. S. Cavalry Association, for the "professional unity and improvement, and the advancement of the cavalry service generally."

The measure of the mounted officers' thirst for status and professional development is evident in their decision to organize an association in the face of many obstacles. Cavalrymen were scattered about the country from the Division of the Atlantic to the Division of the Pacific. In an Army numbering less than 27,000 officers and men, there were but ten regiments of cavalry, containing as potential members of the Association only 424 officers. The regiments were split into small detachments and parcelled out over a remote frontier, charged with such assorted duties as fighting Indians, controlling them on reservations, guarding and operating stage lines, safeguarding settlers, protecting railroads, restricting the depredations of desperadoes and keeping watch over labor disputes — in sum, a police force rather than an army.

Under these circumstances an officer had little hope of finding an opportunity to acquire leadership experience through the command of sizable units in maneuvers (although cavalry officers in particular gained self-reliance in the very fractionalization of their units, which placed a full load of responsibility on officers serving in small isolated commands and far removed from their superiors). And campaigns of a size comparable to that of 1876, when Custer was overwhelmed at Little Big Horn, by 1885 were highly unlikely. For even though General Crook was actively campaigning in Arizona territory against Geronimo and his Chiricahua Apaches, and Wounded Knee was yet five years in the future, this was the twilight of Indian uprising. The officer corps had little choice but to turn to theory to promote professional qualification.

The creators of the Cavalry Association took their problems into account in organizing their society. To contend with the matter of dispersion they established not only the headquarters at Fort Leavenworth, but branches at West Point and in Indian Territory at Fort Reno. They demonstrated a fine touch for the cultivation of higher authority and an alertness to extra-military considerations by conferring honorary membership on the recently retired Commanding General of the Army, William T. Sherman; on Lew Wallace, soldier, lawyer, governor, diplomat and author of *Ben Hur*; on Philip St. George Cooke and William S. Harney, distinguished retired general officers; and on two ex-generals of the Confederacy, Fitzhugh Lee, who became governor or Virginia as the Association was being launched, and "Fightin' Joe" Wheeler, then a member of Congress from the State of Alabama. To these were added John Codman Ropes, distinguished military historian of the day, and Professor Jean Roemer, vice president of City

College of New York and author of *Cavalry, Its History, Management and Uses in War.*

In the matter of active officership of the Association, the founders elected a Medal of Honor winner, Major Abraham K. Arnold, then of 6th Cavalry, as president, and Captain Theodore J. Wint of 4th Cavalry as secretary. The membership would turn to the general officer ranks for Arnold's successor, setting a precedent that holds to this day. But more on the presidents later.

Fort Leavenworth offered auspicious surroundings for the development of professional activity. Here in 1881 Sherman had established the School of Application for Infantry and Cavalry, a great stride forward in the building of a military educational system for the Army. It had been Sherman who sent Emory Upton to Europe and Asia to study the workings of foreign armies, and Upton had confirmed the place of the service school in the development of a professional officer corps. With their mature professionalism, European armies were the object of careful scrutiny in America, where military professionalism was yet in the formative stages. It is not surprising, therefore, that many of the papers presented and discussed in early Cavalry Association meetings turned on the European scene.

The early months of Association activity are somewhat vague due to a paucity of records. A general lack of a sense of history on the part of successive administrations, not limited to the early years, permitted the dissipation of much valuable archival material. The saving feature thus has been the society's publication, which today constitutes a priceless record.

The first issue of the *Journal of the U. S. Cavalry Association* came from the steam press of Kecheson and Reeves at Leavenworth, Kansas, in March of 1888. The preoccupation of the American military with European armies is evident in two articles: "Some German Ideas on Cavalry Gathered from 'Conversations on Cavalry' — Prince Kraft de Hohenlohe-Ingelfingen," and "The French Cavalry: Its Organization, Armament, Remount Service, Schools, Instruction, Drill and Tactics." A great debate of the period — whether the mounted soldier should be armed with saber or revolver, or both — runs through several articles. Other items discuss remounts, a new type field artillery piece, and devices to assist the cavalryman in firing the pistol and carbine efficiently from the back of a horse.

Equally interesting with article content is a list of Association members appearing at the back of Volume I, Number 1. There is Captain Myles Moylan, who commanded A of the 7th Cavalry with the Reno battalion at Little Big Horn. Captain H. W. Lawton, who rendered conspicuous service in bringing Geronimo to heel, and who will die a lieutenant general while serving against Filipino insurgents, is a member. Soldier-author Charles King, progenitor of the Ernest Haycox school of literature, is there. There are Lieutenants W. C. Brown and J. V. S. Paddock, whose names are inscribed respectively in the history of the Sheepeater War in Idaho and the Milk River engagement in Colorado, in 1879. Rufus Fairchild Zogbaum appears — artist and author, faithful delineator of military and naval subjects. And then there is Major and Brevet Colonel Guy V. Henry, holder of the Medal of Honor for action at Cold Harbor in 1864, and severely wounded in the Battle of the Rosebud under George Crook in 1876: Guy V. Henry, who will retire a major general, as will his equally distinguished son, Guy V. Henry, Jr., a future Chief of Cavalry (1930—1934), career member of the Association of the mounted arm, and its president from 1930 to 1934.

Publication of that first list in March 1888 apparently gave the organization a shot in the arm, for the membership jumped from 182 to 310 by June and was pushing 400 in November on the third anniversary of the Association.

Yellowstone Expedition of 1874

Joining up were Frederick W. Benteen, Winfield S. Edgerly and E. S. Godfrey, all of the Benteen battalion at Little Big Horn; Samuel B. M. Young, Adna R. Chaffee, J. Franklin Bell and John J. Pershing, all destined to be Chiefs of Staff of the United States Army; James Parker, another Medal of Honor recipient and a future Association president (1915-1917); and Camillo C. C. Carr, Jacob A. Augur and Ezra B. Fuller, future editors of the *Cavalry Journal*.

In 92 years of publication (1888—1980), 33 officers have held the editorial chair of the *Magazine of Mobile Warfare* as it is sometimes called today. Fifteen have been West Pointers and eight went on to become general officers: Carr, William H. Carter, Charles D. Rhodes, Robert C. Richardson, Jr., Karl S. Bradford, Oliver L. Haines, Charles S. Kilburn, and Fenton S. Jacobs. Of these, Carter, who won the Medal of Honor in Arizona in 1881, holds the distinction of having served the Association in both editorial and executive capacities: he was editor as a captain in the period 1892-1897, and president as a general from 1908 to 1914 and again from 1917 to 1921.

Six of the 38 presidents to date of the mounted society were Chiefs of Cavalry, encompassing the full period of existence of that office from 1920 to 1942: Major Generals Willard Holbrook, Malin Craig, Herbert Crosby, Guy Henry, Leon Kromer, and John Herr. One of these, Malin Craig, was Army Chief of Staff from 1935 to 1939, bridging the tours of Generals MacArthur and Marshall. The trend in presidential rank has been upward through the years, from Major Arnold to Brigadier General Wesley Merritt in the opening years, then up through major general, lieutenant general, and general, with some fluctuation, four stars being the predominant rank of recent years.

All of the presidents of the Association have made significant contributions to the professional society, but it is the second president, Brigadier General Wesley Merritt, who deserves a large share of credit for the success, indeed perpetuation, of the Cavalry Association.

A West Pointer, Class of 1860, Merritt graduated into the Civil War, rising to become a general before the age of 30. Assuming the presidency of the Association in 1887, Merritt was retained by the membership for a 20-year tenure, until his death in January 1908. His great contribution was to give prestige to the organization in the critical years of consolidation. He was largely instrumental in boosting the society over the hurdle caused by the Spanish American War, when all officers except the vice president were at the front, resulting in a single issue of the *Journal* in 1898, four difficult numbers in 1899, and a complete suspension of operations in 1900 and 1901. In an inspirational letter to the membership, Merritt in April 1902 threw his weight behind continuation of the organization and its magazine. "I have been told," he wrote, "by more than one officer whose advancement in the cavalry service has been marked, that much of the success was due to the influence of the studies induced by the Cavalry Association."

The studies to which Merritt referred, those papers presented before various groups of members and as articles in the *Journal*, ranged over a field of subjects of logical interest to the military man, and particularly the mounted soldier: tactics, techniques, training, weapons, doctrine, equipment, organization, horsemanship and horsemastership, education, personalities, and history, to mention some major areas. Discussions were lively and detailed. In the *Journal* for July 1903, for example, 30 officers discoursed on the Johnson bridle bit. To stimulate such professional interest the Association in 1897 had launched an essay contest. Back of a requirement that essays be based on an assigned subject lay a plan to publish a history of the American Cavalry. Although this never materialized, the professional activity engendered by the annual contest inspired the preparation of much good material for the magazine. In the 1903 contest, for instance, a board composed of Generals J. H. Wilson and Fitzhugh Lee and Colonel Arthur L. Wagner (the latter the noted educator at the Leavenworth School), judging material on the basis of historical accuracy, professional excellence, and literary merit, awarded top honors to Captain James G. Harbord for his treatise on "The History of the Cavalry of Northern Virginia (Confederate) During the Civil War." As Harbord's advancement in the service would be marked (he was to rise to Deputy Chief of Staff of the Army), his serves as a case in point in confirmation of General Merritt's remark on the value of Association studies with relation to professional advancement.

With the close of the Spanish American War the United States Army embarked on what has been called the second phase of its Renaissance. In its sphere, the Cavalry Association moved forward. Its gathering professional strength is evidenced in many ways in this period, and not least by the October 1902 membership list, which carries the names of Generals Arthur MacArthur, Leonard Wood, and Tasker Bliss. It was at this time, too, that the *Journal* got a face-lifting from an unexpected source.

Frederic Remington, whose pen and brush contributed so materially to the enduring historical record of our Western frontier, was a life member of the Cavalry Association. In 1898 Remington visited the camp of the 3d Cavalry at Tampa, Florida, where the regiment was staging for the Santiago campaign. The artist, on his way to cover the war in Cuba for *Harper's Weekly*, was a close friend of Captain Francis H. Hardie, who commanded Troop G of the 3d. During the visit Remington's attention was drawn to one of G's noncommissioned officers, Sergeant John Lannen. A superb rider and an imposing figure, the soldier impressed Remington as the perfect example of a cavalryman. He made several rough sketches of Lannen.

From these roughs, Remington later made two finished sketches, which he presented to the Cavalry Association in 1902, as the *Cavalry Journal* was resuming publication. His excellent drawing of a frontier cavalryman appeared on the front cover of the *Journal* in January 1903. It was to hold this position for almost 40 years, until July 1942, and through the years would acquire the label "Old Bill." The second sketch, of a cavalryman riding away from the viewer at a gallop, appeared on the back cover and as a tailpiece inside the magazine for many years. But it was the front cover sketch that had feel, character, authenticity. Always a branch of great *esprit* and highly conscious of history and tradition, the Cavalry took the Remington masterpiece to its heart. It appears to this day in the professional magazine of the mounted arm, a trademark of mobility in war.

As the impact of the Army's renaissance and the Cavalry Association's example became increasingly felt, other branch associations and magazines began to appear on the military scene. Many officers of Infantry, Artillery and other services had joined the Cavalry Association, drawn by a community of professional interest. Inevitably a desire for greater concentration on branch affairs intruded, and the various specialists took steps to form their own organizations. The year 1892 saw the creation of the Coast Artillery Association and magazine. Infantrymen launched an organization in 1893 and a journal in 1904. Field Artillerymen put their society under way in 1910, and between 1920 and 1946 the services lined up — Engineers, Ordnance, Quartermaster, Transportation, Signal and Chemical. These organizations and their "trade journals of war" over the years have rendered a clear service to the Army and the nation. Since passage of the National Security Act of 1947, most have expanded to cover their subject areas on a Defense-wide basis.

With the 20th Century came mechanization. Its

application to military purposes had broad implications, especially for the Cavalry arm. As the tank moved on to the battlefields of World War I its element of protection was in the ascendant, for it was designed to breach the trench stalemate by overcoming the machine gun and barbed wire. Yet it was an augury for the future when General Pershing placed the Tank Corps under the command of a cavalryman, Brigadier General Samuel D. Rockenbach, longtime member of the Cavalry Association and a contributor to the *Journal*'s pages as far back as 1894. One of his younger officers was Captain George S. Patton, Jr., who a quarter-century later in another global conflict would do so much with this machine which he helped introduce to the battlefield. Incidentally, the careful researcher in the *Cavalry Journal* may trace the career of Association member Patton through articles under his byline ranging from lieutenant to general and spanning three decades.

World War I brought another crisis in Cavalry Association affairs. The secretary-treasurer-editor, retired Lieutenant Colonel Fuller, in poor health but carrying on, was awaiting replacement. But as Fuller noted in the July 1917 issue of the *Journal*, "everybody who can wants to go to war, and those who can't don't want the job." He suggested that it might be better to suspend operations as had been the case at the turn of the century. But he got out three more issues, and with the April 1918 number the *Cavalry Journal* went into suspense for two years, with 1919 a complete blank.

As it had on the occasion of the other interruption, the *Journal* came out of this one with a new face. Old Bill still graced the cover, but page size was expanded and layout revamped. Major Robert C. Richardson, Jr. moved into the chair in replacement of Fuller. And now the Association's base of operations was moved to Washington, D. C. The organization had need to be on the scene in the Nation's Capital, for its future, inextricably interwoven with the future of the Cavalry, was by no means definitely assured. As Major LeRoy Eltinge put it in the April 1920 revival issue, "the Cavalry of the Army emerged from the World War in poorer condition than any arm of the service." Indeed, there was much to be done.

That issue opened fittingly enough with an inspirational message to the Cavalry from General John J. Pershing, designed to carry the arm through critical times. The theme running through the number was hopeful: "the future of cavalry lies in its mobility."

It was in this period that the Army, recognizing the real contribution of the unofficial professional associations and journals to the profession of arms, authorized the assignment of active duty personnel to the editorial—secretarial posts; the task up to this time had been carried out in their spare time by a small number of highly dedicated officers. Under the new arrangement the organizations rightfully retained their freedom of operation, although in the '30s they lost the revenue of advertisers when Congress wrote into the appropriations bill a rider prohibiting publications run by active duty staffs from taking paid advertising — a far cry from those years in the '80s and '90s when the *Journal* carried a lively advertisers' section; when the ads were oozing with testimonials and even the Post Chaplain at Fort Leavenworth was delighted to give his endorsement to Woodley's *Sans Pareil,* the Great Army Remedy for the Preservation of the Hair!

At the close of World War I the thinking with respect to employment of the tank was still far from clear. There was indecision as to which of the ground arms should have cognizance over development. The Tank Corps was dissolved and tank development placed under the Chief of Infantry. The general theory of mechanization, however, was assigned to the Cavalry. Few professionals yet saw the possibilities inherent in armor — that Cavalry might logically inherit armor, and that armor possessed the classic cavalry characteristics of mobility, firepower and shock action, and therefore the capability of carrying on the cavalry role. Daniel Van Voorhis, Adna R. Chaffee, Jr., and a few more spoke out. But the horse had an attraction to the heart as well as the head of the cavalryman, and even at the time in the '30s when the 7th Cavalry Brigade (Mechanized) was formed, it was generally considered to be a professional hazard for an officer to identify himself with the new medium. Few cavalrymen were prepared to trade the horse for the tank and perhaps compromise their careers. Among those who stepped to the new field, however, were two future presidents of the mounted society, I. D. White and Willis C. Crittenberger.

Through these years of growing pains the Cavalry Association gave some attention to mechanization through the pages of the *Journal*, but more to horses. Gradually the article had taken the place of the paper of earlier times. The Association became essentially its magazine, and there through the '30s many of the big names of World War II put in an appearance, and not all were cavalrymen: Jonathan M. Wainwright, Lucien K. Truscott, Joseph W. Stilwell, Maurice Rose, Robert W. Grow; and in 1931, Major Dwight D. Eisenhower, authoring an article on "War Policies."

As war flared once again in Europe, the crisis developing in the Army over the Cavalry role deepened. Events came to a head with a rush. In 1940 the Army bypassed the traditional ground arms by organizing an Armored Force, while at the same time in the Cavalry famous horse regiments were partially and then completely mechanized. In 1942 the offices of the Chiefs of the Combat Arms (Cavalry, Infantry, Artillery) were abolished. As a crowning blow to the Cavalry, the famous First Cavalry Division was dismounted and sent to the Southwest Pacific as a foot unit.

A hint of the struggle attendant upon these events is

apparent in the words of Major General John K. Herr, last Chief of Cavalry (1938-1942), and president of the Cavalry Association from 1939 to 1945. The quotation is from his book, *The Story of the U. S. Cavalry* (Little Brown & Co., Boston, 1953), written with Edward S. Wallace and published not long before his death:

> What caused this sudden and extreme action? It was probably a combination of factors. The great successes of the German panzers (which nobody denied) over the good roads in the flat country of northern Europe had their effect on the extremely motor-conscious American public and its tendency to rush *en masse* to extremes. The horse was dead! Long live the motor! Thus reasoned many people who had never tried to cut cross country, between the hard roads, in their shiny, chromium-plated, streamlined pride of the Detroit production line and knew nothing about the use of horses. That there was influence brought to bear by certain industries which would profit heavily by the production of the enormously expensive tank and other mechanized vehicles is almost certain. Then, there was the ever-eternal green-eyed monster of jealousy which had been aroused in the breasts of the other services, especially among soft and inactive officers behind desks, over the color and glamour attached to the cavalry, over the good times which officers of that branch enjoyed in their sports at all the cavalry posts, and over the certain indefinable social prestige which the man on horseback, the cavalier, the *hidalgo,* the gentleman, has always had over the man on foot. All these influences combined, and amidst the excitement at the outbreak of war, managed to eliminate what they called an archaic branch.

Whatever the reasons, the horse departed the Army, and the mounted arm was beset by internal divisions that threatened its professional base. The Cavalry Association suffered as well, and partly by its own hand.

With the U. S. Army at its wartime peak in strength, the *Infantry Journal* soared to well over 100,000 subscriptions exclusive of the Overseas Edition. Not so the *Cavalry Journal*. Against a potential represented by 16 armored divisions full of cavalrymen, a cavalry division, many armored cavalry groups and squadrons, and many separate tank and tank destroyer units, the *Cavalry Journal* reached a subscription peak of little more than 7,000. This can be attributed to a failure to break with the past and step out resolutely to embrace the new medium — armor — which had absorbed the great percentage of branch members. As German panzer forces lashed out across European battlefields, Russian horse cavalry galloped across *Cavalry Journal* pages. Armor and mechanization got some space, but a provisional platoon of horse-mounted soldiers in the Italian campaign was likely to receive equal attention with the exploits of an American armored division. And there was continuing attention to foreign horse cavalry, horsebreeding, and equestrian sports. The Association lost many sincere professionals from its membership rolls.

In World War II the Cavalry Association and *Cavalry Journal* met a war which did not put operations at least temporarily on ice. But in clinging to the past the Association came close to sealing its own doom. The low point was late 1947, when subscriptions dropped to around 1,800. One step of importance had recently been taken which might redeem a bad situation. In mid-1946 a small group of professionals had rallied round and put the organization in tune with realities. The name was changed to U. S. *Armored* Cavalry Association. The magazine became *Armored Cavalry Journal*. Content increasingly reflected the new order.

In all fairness it must be noted that all service journals suffered a share of the difficulties growing out of the postwar ebb. The league-leading *Infantry Journal*, feeling the subscription pinch, in the late '40s put forward a merger proposal which in essence suggested the liquidation of the Associations and journals of Cavalry, Field Artillery and Coast (Antiaircraft) Artillery, with all assets to be turned over to a new organization and magazine of Army-wide implication and title, based on the Infantry Association's existing plant and staff, with some minor representation of the other three organizations. By 1953 the two Artillery organizations had joined this Association of the U. S. Army in the *Combat Forces Journal* (today *Army*). The members of the Armored Cavalry Association voted down the proposition, seeing it as a sub-merger, and desiring to retain a strong voice in behalf of their troubled branch. The Association position was admirably represented by Lieutenant General Geoffrey Keyes in high-level meetings with advocates of a merger of the several combat arms magazines and societies. From initial negotiations in 1948 through 1952 editorial expression and later reaffirmation by Executive Council resolution, the mounted organization consistently supported the concept of an Army-wide Association, while maintaining a firm stand in behalf of branch societies and journals. A sentiment for perpetuation, it may be noted parenthetically, was not unusual for an organization with a lineage such as that of the mounted society. Many military families may be traced through the history of the mounted organization and the pages of its publication, from distinguished father to distinguished son. The Cavalry family tree is liberally sprinkled with the accomplishments of several generations of Henrys and Howzes, Holbrooks, Reads and Pattons, to note a few examples.

Mid-century will go down in the history of the society of the mounted arm and its publication as a moment of resurrection. For it was then that Congress passed the Army Organization Act of 1950. The legislation made of record an evolution which had been in process for several decades. The passage that cleared the air read: *The Armor shall be a continuation of the Cavalry.*

The steps remaining to be taken were obvious, and the Association's Executive Council moved immediately to implement them. On the heels of the legislative action the Armored Cavalry Association became the U. S. Armor Association. The magazine became simply *Armor*. The July-August 1950 issue came out re-designed from cover to cover, setting a style which won for the publication national certificates of award in the Magazine Shows of 1951 and 1952, sponsored by the American Institute of Graphic Arts. New features and top authorship and material greatly enhanced the magazine's reputation.

A year and a half later the society, breaking the precedent of 25-member annual meetings in one room of Washington's Army and Navy Club, moved to Fort Knox, the Home of Armor, for its annual reunion. As many officers attended the business session in Theater No. 1 as had been on duty in the ten regiments of cavalry existing in the Army when the society was launched at Fort Leavenworth 66 years before.

In spite of that revitalization, the Association and its magazine had to remain flexible and adapt to shifting conditions. The highly workable situation under which a perceptive Army permitted active duty staffs to run a semi-official organization and magazine because of the professional value of the activity, almost inevitably came to an end. Over the course of several decades, through a gradual process of transition, consolidation, and voluntary relinquishment, the staffs of a number of professional societies and journals became civilianized, and each move, prompted by multi-service, industrial, and commercial considerations, left the remaining organizations more unique, exposed, and vulnerable. Active duty staffs eventually became a luxury in a period of retrenchment. Thus in 1973 the Army announced that active duty military personnel would no longer be assigned to professional but unofficial branch associations and journals. Within that policy framework, however, the Army still recognized the cogent background reasons that had supported the practice for half a century.

The Armor Association's Executive Council met to consider how it might sustain the organization's appreciable professional role within the framework of the new policy. As a result, the Association's role as publisher of the magazine was discontinued. *Armor* was moved to Fort Knox, Kentucky, to become an official publication of the U. S. Army Armor School. Association members continued to receive the magazine as their professional branch organ, and the organization maintained its role by continuing to sponsor the annual professional conference devoted to armor. Thus both the organization and the magazine continue today as strong and vital professional activities of a strong and vital combat arm of the Army.

Perhaps the outcome for a society beset by many difficulties was foreordained. For after all, these were events affecting the mounted soldier, the *arme blanche*, CAVALRYMEN! The sense of all this has perhaps never been put more effectively than by a non-cavalryman. Writing from Tokyo in 1948 in observance of the *Cavalry Journal's* sixtieth anniversary of service devoted to "keeping the military profession abreast of the cavalry arm in the art of war," General of the Army Douglas MacArthur said: "During these decades no other branch has experienced greater change in weapons, in technique, and in tactical requirement. Discarding the horse and the saber to keep pace with the increasing tempo and violence of modern war, the cavalryman speedily adjusted himself to armored mechanization and commensurate firepower, firmly to hold his historic role of the far-flung and rapid movement echelon. In this he demonstrated with striking clarity that the invincible *esprit* which has characterized his past yet carries him to the vanguard of every advance, an irresistible force toward victory."

— William Gardner Bell

Foreword

For some inexplicable reason, the Yellowstone Expedition of 1873 has been the least reported of all of Custer's military experiences, far less than the Black Hills Expedition the following year. And I cannot explain this. Certainly the 1873 trip had more exciting adventures with Indians what with two notable skirmishes; the 1874 trip produced none of consequence. I suppose the confirmation of gold in the Black Hills generated more excitement than just a railroad survey, but it was the confirmation of gold which brought the country some good economic news and regenerated our push westward, while the railroad survey had been halted in 1873 because of the declining economic picture and the subsequent recession which stunted much of our growth for a very long time. It is interesting to note that Custer figured prominently in both instances. And then, there was no General Stanley[1] in 1874.

In determining the thrust of this Foreword, several approaches and subjects were outlined and then discarded. And then, since the presence of General Stanley in 1873 made the major difference, it was decided to focus on the Stanley-Custer feud, and even with this decision, far too little physical evidence existed. Most of it appeared in personal letters and as a consequence the story had to be pieced together.

First of all, the Northern Pacific Railroad had experienced trouble with Stanley on the previous year's survey.

> "Rosser has told me how badly General S. behaved last year, some days being so overcome the expedition could not go

on. One morning the engineers started at the appointed hour, but Rosser, looking back from a high bluff, saw that the infantry camp was still standing. On going back he found the officers searching for the General, but in vain. Finally, Major Worth told Rosser confidentially that, having found Genl. S. dead drunk on the ground outside the camp, he had carried him into his own tent, though he and the General were not on good terms, for the honor of the service. He was then lying there in a drunken stupor.

"Rosser said he told General S. in St. Paul before starting that he would have a different man to deal with this year, in command of the 7th, — one who would not hesitate, as second in command, to put a guard over him, S., if incapacitated. Genl. S., Rosser said, acknowledged that he knew this and would try to do better. But whiskey has too strong a hold on him."[2]

It is important to establish the fact Stanley was a heavy drinker, so heavy, in fact, that it did influence his military performance. Custer did not drink. These two facts alone were enough to set the stage for the drama which was to unfold.

Just where the original of the substantive feud can be pinpointed is difficult to establish. However, with "friends" like Theodore Goldin[3] working behind the scenes, it's not that hard to determine.

"You may have heard or possibly read, of a rumor that was in circulation at Lincoln, even before the expedition left there, of a statement said to have been made by Custer, who was known to have felt chagrined that he was not sent out at the head of this expedition. This statement was to the effect that if the opportunity offered he would give Terry the slip as he had given it to Stanley in '73 . . . "[4]

The letter in which this statement appeared concerned the 1876 Campaign, but the inference of Custer's disrespectful disobedience was there for all to read. And it is even acknowledged as being only a rumor! But the anti-Custer writers have had a field day with this, reading into it almost anything they wished — even in the face of a lack of substantiation — and whenever the differences between Custer and Stanley surfaced, this statement was to serve as their main source in their interpretation of Custer's behavior.

That is certainly flimsy evidence, but obviously enough where the Custer detractors were concerned. An example of this is:

> "He [Custer] strove to dominate General Stanley on the Yellowstone Expedition until that surly old war-dog turned upon him savagely. Thereafter Custer was contrite and obedient."[5]

And then, if that were not enough one-sided interpretation, again:

> "Thereafter, as always when reproof had been swift, severe and certain, Custer was contrite and placating... Throughout the expedition's long march, he was Stanley's eager and respectful subordinate."[6]

These are strong and powerful words, and used incorrectly. They do not adequately describe an accurate picture of the total story. Not once is Stanley's drunken behavior mentioned. Not once did that author attempt to analyze Custer's actions in a situation not unlike a ship in a stormy sea without a Captain. That is tragic, and the only purpose it served was the perpetuation of a half-truth based on a rumor repeated by an enlisted man who may or may not have had access to the whole story at any time. This is dangerous history!

But the feud did exist, almost a mutual mistrust as Stanley wrote to his wife:

> "There will be a certain amount of trouble which I think I can encounter and conquer..."[7]

Then later he wrote:

> "...I have had no trouble with Custer; and will try to avoid having any; but I have seen enough of him to convince me that he is a cold blooded, untruthful and unprincipled man.
> "He is universally despised by all the officers of his regiment excepting his relatives and one or two sycophants. He brought a trader in the field without permission, carries an old Negro woman, a cast iron cooking stove, and delays the march often by his extensive packing up in the morning. As I said, I will try, but I am not sure I can avoid trouble with him..."[8]

Then, in another letter to his wife, Stanley wrote:

> ". . . I had a little flurry with Custer as I told you I probably would. We were separated 4 miles, and I intended him to assist in getting the train, his own train, over the Muddy River. Without consulting me he marched off 15 miles, coolly sending me a note to send him forage and rations. I sent after him, ordered him to halt where he was, to unload his wagons, send for his own rations and forage, and never to presume to make another movement without orders.
>
> "I knew from the start that it had to be done, and I am glad to have so good a chance, when there could be no doubt who was right. He was just gradually assuming command, and now he knows he has a commanding officer who will not tolerate his arrogance . . ."[9]

Evidently Stanley felt his little chastisement over a little and insignificant act would solve all his own problems, for he wrote his wife:

> ". . . Custer, who by the way has behaved very well, since he agreed to do so, went ahead every day to look up road and select best camps . . ."[10]

Custer also was a prolific letter writer. In one to his wife he wrote:

> "Our officers are terribly down on him [Stanley]. One day, when intoxicated. after leaving Rice, he abused Mr. Baliran in such coarse terms, calling him foul names . . . and threatened to hang him, should he seek to come into camp at any time."[11]

There are a few points in the Stanley letters to be cleared up. First, I do not think Custer was "universally despised by all the officers of his regiment." There is absolutely no basis in fact for this statement. It is possible Custer was not liked by many on one occasion or another, and usually when a decision of some kind or another is made unfavorable to the individual, but to state that which Stanley did in no uncertain terms is patently untrue. A good example of fluctuating admiration is Albert Barnitz. His opinion fluttered in the wind and changed almost as often as did the wind, but the change was almost always identified with something done unfavorably to him. Whenever something was done which he liked, his attitude then changed to one of favor for Custer.[12]

Another point brought up in Stanley's letters was the reference to the trader, Mr. Baliran.[13] Never once does Stanley refer to this man in his official reports. And peculiarly, Stanley was disturbed because Mr. Baliran carried whiskey. It is difficult to understand this attitude when all one has to do is check the records to find Stanley was too often "in his cups." Was he afraid of his own weakness? Did Mr. Baliran represent a temptation which Stanley felt he could not face or overcome?

There are two versions of the Baliran episode which bear presentation here.

> "I know the third day out from Rice, that Col. Fred Grant informed Custer that on next day a search of the whole train was to be made; train halted enroute for whiskey. Baliran's whiskies and wines were put in the 7th Cavalry troop wagons and Baliran's wagons carried grain belonging to some troops. Ketchum and Ray, A.C. & C.S. for Stanley, evidently did not inform Fred Grant of the fact that they were going to swoop down on the store in camp of 7th, or they might have been spirited away; but with the earliest dawn, the two members of Stanley's staff came, axes in hand, and spilt the good red liquor on the dry alkaline soil of Montana at the 'Stockade' camp.
>
> "Grant, Gibson, Weston and myself had procured a quart about one-half hour before destruction. We were owling! Now Stanley was stupidly drunk at the time, and that is how Custer got away with it."[14]

The other version was written by Custer:

> "Genl. S. in one of his fits of ill-humor, ordered Col. Grant to go to the 7th Cavalry, and inspect Mr. Baliran's wagons and stores, and, if he found any spirituous liquors there, to take an axe and spill the contents of barrels. This would have injured Mr. B. financially, as he had thousands of dollars worth in hand. Col. Grant was greatly mortified, but fortunately Mr. B's wagons were so far in the rear it was hours before they arrived. So, after chatting with me on pleasant topics Col. Grant said, 'Well, my tent leaked last night, so I guess I will go back and take a nap. By that time the wagons may be in. And I hope the sutler will have anything of the kind hidden before I come to inspect.'
>
> "Our officers regarded Genl. S's orders as persecution, and were eager to help. So Mr. B. loaded his drinkables into one wagon and made the rounds of our temperate officers, leaving with each a keg of brandy, case of rum, a barrel of Bourbon, for temporary keeping. Never were temperate officers so well provided with intoxicants. Then Genl. S.

reconsidered, cancelled his order to Col. Grant to inspect. But, fearing this might be a trap, the officers retained the kegs, etc., for a few days, till the excitement was over."[15]

The whole truth must be somewhere within the two narratives. Custer did not mention the spilling of liquor, and Benteen did not mention that which was saved. Perhaps most of the truth has not been compromised, but had it not been for these two letters, no evidence of that episode would ever have surfaced. Since the sutler's store was outside the camp proper, and since Mr. Baliran was on the trip as a guest of the officers, General Stanley did act out of line and improperly. One of the most telling points is the fact the officers so distrusted Stanley that they even feared he was plotting against them; they feared his action was a trap. All the officers cannot be paranoid, so some of Stanley's real character is innocently and truthfully exposed.

Stanley's continued bout with the bottle cost the expedition much in the way of delays. Custer wrote Elizabeth:

"Yesterday we marched at noon, but only five miles before going into camp. Everybody is chafing at the delay. We have been thirteen days at one point when three would have sufficed. Whiskey alone is the cause. You have no idea how this has delayed the expedition and added to the government expenses. The steamer has been detained here needlessly for ten days, at $500 a day — $5000. Genl. Rosser says it is a disgrace to the service."[16]

Stanley never mentioned this, nor did anyone else in their official papers. However, George D. Wallace,[17] a young Second Lieutenant newly assigned to the 7th Cavalry, wrote a letter to his father in which he stated almost the same about delays:

"... The trip could have been made in half the time. There is one thing might be investigated. A boat has accompanied the command. While in motion they simply charge for freight, but while tied to the bank they get $20.00 per hour.

This explains why Custer makes such short marches. I do not say he shares in the profit, but if he was working to the interest of the gov't we might have been at Ft. Rice several days ago. If he was jerked up about it he would claim that he was working for the good of the service by making short marches, but *that is a little too thin.*"[18]

Poor Custer! He can't win for losing. Though he had to march over mostly difficult terrain along with his whole command, and still keep the freight boat in sight — which was on the river in June, high water time — he was forced to move much slower than his usual pace. Young Wallace, new to the frontier, did not take all factors into consideration and wrote very damaging observations about Custer, damaging if they had been released outside the family. So here is Custer receiving criticism from a young subordinate, who didn't know what he was talking about, and being detained on the march by a drunken superior officer. No wonder he was chomping at the bits!

In early July, the relationship between Custer and Stanley hit rock bottom. It wasn't over Stanley's drunkenness, nor over Custer's easy going attitude about the drinking and gambling by the officers within his own command — and Custer did neither on this trip. It was over a horse. This provided the most explosive moment on the whole expedition. Benteen tells it this way:

"On our trip of '73, with Stanley, Custer got Rosser to give Fred Calhoun[19] a job which necessitated Calhoun's being mounted. H Troop was short of horses. Custer had a claybank horse for which I was responsible and which I had assiduously endeavored to have returned to troop, but without avail.

"Lieutenant Ray,[20] Commissary of expedition, from lack of horses, had to content himself with riding a poor mule from his train, so Ray said to me one day, 'Benteen, can you not do better for me than this?'

"'Yes, I think I can,' I said. 'Now I have fourteen dismounted men in troop, but you see that claybank? Well, I'm responsible to U.S. for him, and cannot get him. Custer gives him to that young man [Calhoun] to ride, and now he is employed by Gen. Rosser for the N.P. Get the horse if you can.'

"The correspondence about the horse got Custer in arrest. Stanley got drunk, so the game was thrown into Custer's hand, and thus he got away with Stanley."[21]

Good old Freddie Benteen. He was always good for trouble. Rather than doing anything in a military manner, even approaching Custer first, or even keeping his mouth shut as a subordinate officer should, he, maliciously I do believe, elected to take the steps which he did, knowing full well in advance the friction it would cause, though probably not knowing the full consequences of his behavior beforehand. Even had he known, I'm not certain it would have caused him to perform any differently. Benteen — the burr under Custer's saddle — should have been made to accept full responsibility for that which later transpired, for he was fully to blame. But he escaped official reprimand, as he was to do time and again. The official story is this:

Stanley demanded a horse for Lieutenant Ray; it was to be given up from Custer's command. Custer sent an unacceptable horse. This action resulted in the following Special Order:

Special Order #9   Hqrs. Yellowstone Exp.
Camp No. 13   July 6, 1873

X   X   X   X   X   X

111. The commanding officer Battalion 7th Cavalry, will immediately upon receipt of this order return to the Company Commander properly responsible one dun horse, the property of the United States now used and heretofore ridden in violation of law and regulations by a citizen named Calhoun. The Commanding Officer Battalion 7th Cavalry will report his action in this matter to these headquarters.

X   X   X   X   X   X

V. Captain F. W. Benteen, 7th Cavalry, Company A, will send one serviceable horse to these headquarters for the temporary use of the Chief Commissary of this Expedition.

By Order Of
Col. D. S. Stanley[22]

Custer reviewed the order and complied, sending a horse which displeased Stanley. Stanley, in a violent burst of anger, influenced no doubt by liquor and a smoldering dislike and distrust of Custer caused by his own inadequacies, placed Custer under arrest for what he deemed at the time to be an affront. Totally bewildered, Custer wrote the following to Stanley:

> Headquarters
> Detachment 7th Cavalry
> Camp in the Field, D. T.
> July 9th, 1873

Acting Assistant Adjutant General
Yellowstone Expedition

Your communication of this date in which you refer to the horse furnished by order of the Colonel Commanding, has just been received, and it is with equal regret and surprise that I learn that the sending of said horse was looked upon by the Colonel Commanding as an act of disrespect. I greatly regretted at the time my inability to provide a *serviceable* horse, but without violating par 1143 Rev. Army Regulations which prohibits dismounting a trooper to provide a horse for an officer or designating a horse ridden by an officer I was forced to send the horse I did or none at all, that one being the only one not assigned in this command. Each officer of the 7th Cavalry is permitted to ride one public horse in addition to his private horses, this is in accordance with a decision of a former Dept. Commander (Major General Hancock then commanding Department of the Missouri). The horse ridden by Mr. Calhoun was a public horse that I had appropriated for my own use, he having been previously ridden by the Wagonmaster of this Battalion. Mr. Calhoun only rode him a few days and then considered him as a temporary loan from me, I informing him that while we were making such easy marches I would not require the use of this horse. In sending the horse which was afterwards returned I claim to have acted in good faith to all concerned, to my Commanding Officer and to those under me. It would have been far more satisfactory to me had I been able to have furnished not only a serviceable horse but a superior one, could I have done so without both violating regulations and interfering with what I believed were the rights of those under me. Nothing was farther from my intention than to do ought which would admit of being construed as an act of disrespect. Furthermore, in conversation with Lieut. Ray in regard to supplying him with a horse, previous to receiving an order to that effect, I fully explained to him the absolute scarcity of horses in this command and expressed my regret at my inability to furnish him with a suitable mount. Further than this I sent 1st Lieut. A. E. Smith, 7th Cavy., to personally explain the same matter to the Colonel Commanding. He returned and reported that the explanation was understood and seemed satisfactory. In regard to the return of the order referred to I would state that full twenty-four hours previous to my interview with the Colonel Commanding, I had caused an official copy of the order, verified by me, to be filed with the records of these Headqrs., hence did not regard the sending of the original copy with endorsements as a departure from what was proper.

> Respectfully yours,
> G. A. CUSTER
> Lieut. Col. 7th Cavy."[23]

Nothing could be more clear. Custer even had record of that which transpired. Stanley was clearly in the wrong, and it is evident Custer had far more respect for the welfare of his own men than did Stanley. Oddly, Custer is very often accused of just the opposite, but most often by writers who know only one side of a story and are satisfied with what they know.

On the same day the letter was written, Stanley had Custer released from arrest, and Custer was ordered to report to him. There was no special order either placing him in or relieving him from arrest. And so ended the affair between the supposedly headstrong Custer and the besotten Stanley. Stanley refrained from reporting any of the foregoing in either his official or private papers or letters. Perhaps he was just as happy to have it forgotten. Custer, magnanimously, mentioned it only once in a letter to Elizabeth:

"In regard to my arrest and its attendant circumstances, I am sorry it ever reached your ears, as I hoped — not for myself, but those who were the cause of it, that the matter should end here.

"Suffice to say that I was placed in arrest for acting in strict conscientious discharge of what I knew to be my duty — a duty laid down expressly in Army Regulations.

"Never was I more confident of the rectitude of my course, and of the official propriety of my position . . . so confident that I was content to wait, knowing that I would be vindicated in the end.

"Within forty-eight hours Genl. Stanley came to me, and apologized in the most ample manner, acknowledging that he had been in the wrong, hoping I would forget it, and promising to turn over a new leaf.

"Twice did he repeat 'I humbly beg your pardon, sir. I do not only make this apology to you, but, if you desire it, will gladly do so in the presence of your officers.'

"With his subsequent faithful observance of his promise to begin anew in his intercourse with me, I banished the affair from my mind. Nor do I cherish any but the kindliest sentiments towards him, for Genl. Stanley, when not possessed by the fiend of intemperance, is one of the kindest, most agreeable and considerate officers I ever served under.

"Looking back I regard it, as do other officers, as a necessity that an issue was forced on us, and that by my opposing, instead of yielding, the interests of the service were advanced. On one occasion whiskey was destroyed by friends of Genl. Stanley as the only means of getting him sober. This was publicly avowed. It had no connection with my difficulty with him, although the papers have coupled the two incidents together.

"Since my arrest complete harmony exists between Genl. Stanley and myself. He frequently drops in at my headquarters and adopts every suggestion I make."[24]

Both officers are of the impression they were the ones to have acted correctly, but Custer is the only one who cited army regulations to back him up. It seems as if both wanted to justify their actions more to their wives than to anyone else, and in so doing, Custer was far more generous in his comments about Stanley, than Stanley was ever to be about Custer.

Not only does Custer explain away the difficulties with Stanley in this one letter, he inadvertently exposes one of the hazards of being a celebrity, the newspapers. They then, as now, seem more interested in fiction than in fact. Here, also is another explanation of why the whiskey was spilled. Benteen suggested other hidden reasons, and Stanley said nothing, which is typical of those at fault. The only time Stanley alludes to this episode is when he writes his wife that he thought Custer had behaved very well since his chastisement. Custer wrote his wife the same about Stanley.

In a departure from his attitudes exposed in his letters to his wife, Stanley frequently went out of his way to single out Custer and his performance on this expedition. This may have been an attempt to expiate his own failings.

Less generously, Custer had this to say as he and the 7th Cavalry parted from Stanley's command:

> "I left General Stanley with the balance of the expedition on the other side of the Yellowstone, enjoying a spree."[25]

Perhaps there are two possible interpretations of this statement, but armed with the knowledge of that which had transpired the previous weeks, it is suggested Stanley had not yet reformed and demon rum was his frequent companion.

The differences between Custer and Stanley were many, but the one major difference which seems to stand out was Custer's farsightedness, an attribute which was to surface again after the 1874 Expedition to the Black Hills and made evident in the continued Custer-Hazen debates on the relative worth of the northwest. Farsightedness seemed to have been an attribute not keenly looked upon the in army in the last century, but this was exactly what made Custer's contributions so remarkable, a military man with strong feelings of humanism. After this expedition he was to write:

> "So earnest is my belief in the civilizing and peace-giving influence of railroads when extended through an Indian country, that the idea has often occurred to me, laying aside all considerations and arguments as to whether such a road will ever be required in the interest of trade and commerce, that a railroad established and kept in operation from a point on one extreme northern boundary somewhere between the 100th and 105th meridian, to a corresponding point on

the Rio Grande sides in Texas, would for ever after have preserved peace with the number of tribes infesting the immense area of country lying between the Rocky Mountains and the valley of the Mississippi. A more surprising statement than this, however, and one which will bear investigation, is that the avoidance of wars with the tribes which have occupied this region of the plains lying contiguous to the indicated line of railroad, would have resulted in a saving of money to the Gov't. more than sufficient to build, equip, and place in running order a railroad from British America to the Rio Grande."[26]

All the foregoing serves only as a foreword to the main narratives in this chapter, the two articles appearing in *Cavalry Journal* regarding the Yellowstone Expedition. The author of the afterword will give an overview of the expedition. When read together it will be possible to have a better understanding of this little-known period in Custer's career, particularly about the personalities who made it so very exciting for historians today. One word of caution. Baliran's name is variously spelled throughout. I have followed the spelling in each case as it appeared in the original.

JOHN M. CARROLL
General Editor

Footnotes

1 See footnote number 21 in following article.

2 Merington, Marguerite, *The Custer Story*, p. 251. This was a letter from Custer to Elizabeth, dated June 1873, D. T.

3 Theodore Goldin was in the hilltop and valley fights at the Little Big Horn. Born on 25 July 1858, his real name being John Stilwell, he enlisted in the 7th Cavalry as a minor. On 21 December 1895, upon his own application, he was awarded the Medal of Honor because of his performance as one of the battle water party who brought water to the wounded on Reno Hill. He participated in a long series of letters with the retired Captain Benteen, the source of so very much in-sight into the personalities of the 7th Cavalry. Goldin died on 15 February 1935. (Hammer, Kenneth, *Biographies of the 7th Cavalry*, Old Army Press, 1972, p. 143; Carroll, John M., ed., *The Benteen-Goldin Letters*, Liveright Publ. Co., 1974, pp. 189-305.)

4 Carroll, John M. ed., *The Benteen-Goldin Letters*, p. 5. This was a letter from Goldin to Brininstool, dated 26 December 1927.

5 Stewart, Edgar I., *Custer's Luck*, p. 178.

6 ibid., p. 243.

7 Stanley, David S., *Memoirs*, p. 238. This was a letter from General Stanley to his wife, dated 12 June 1873.

8 ibid, p. 239. This is a letter from General Stanley to his wife, dated 28 June 1873.

9 ibid, p. 240. This is a letter from General Stanley to his wife, dated 1 July 1873.

10 ibid, p. 241. This is a letter from General Stanley to his wife, dated 15 August 1873.

11 Merington, op, cit., p. 251. This is a letter from Custer to Elizabeth, dated June, 1873, D. T.

12 One has only to read the one major book based on the letters of Albert Barnitz to understand this statement. (Utley, Robert M., ed., *Life In Custer's Cavalry*, Yale University Press, 1977). Barnitz' personal

Yellowstone Expedition of 1874

opinion of Custer changed with the weather. The influencing factor seemed to have been Barnitz' own personal comfort. Barnitz' began his military career as a Sergeant in Compay G, 2nd Ohio Cavalry, on 22 August 1861. By June 1862, he was a commissioned officer and by 1865 he was a Major. He was mustered out that same year, but on 28 July 1866, he was appointed a Captain in the 7th U. S. Cavalry, and was severely wounded in the Battle of the Washita on 27 November 1868. Because of the severity of this wound he retired from the service on 15 December 1870. He did receive, after retirement, a brevet rank of Colonel for this action. (Heitman, Francis B., *Historical Register and Dictionary of the U. S. Army*, p. 193.)

[13] More biographical information on this gentleman appears in the major portion of this text.

[14] Carroll, op. cit., p. 256. This was a letter from Benteen to Goldin, dated 12 February 1896.

[15] Merington, op. cit. pp. 252-53. This was a letter from Custer to Elizabeth, dated June, 1873, D. T.

[16] ibid, p. 260. This was a letter from Custer to Elizabeth, dated July 25, 1873, from the Yellowstone River, Dakota Territory.

[17] George Daniel Wallace of South Carolina. He graduated from the United States Military Academy on 14 June 1872, and was immediately assigned to the 7th U. S. Cavalry, but served in garrison at Newberry, South Carolina, and Memphis, Tennessee, until 10 April 1873; he did not join his command in the field until then. His first service on the frontier was on this expedition. Subsequently, he was to serve on the Black Hills Expedition in 1874, and was engaged in the Battle of the Little Big Horn in 1876, and was killed in the Battle of Wounded Knee on 29 December 1890, at the age of 44. (Carroll, John M. & Price, Byron, ed., *Roll Call On The Little Big Horn*, p. 111.)

[18] This is a letter from Lieutenant Wallace to his father, from the field on the Yellowstone Expedition, dated 8 June 1873. It is in this editor's private collection.

[19] Fred Calhoun was a brother to Lieutenant James Calhoun, a brother-in-law to Custer. Fred was in no way related to Custer.

[20] See footnote number 49 in following article.

[21] Carroll, op. cit. p. 240. This was a letter from Benteen to Goldin, dated 19 January 1896.

[22] Special Order Book, Yellowstone Expedition, National Archives.

[23] Letters Sent and Received, 7th U. S. Cavalry, Yellowstone Expedition, National Archives.

[24] Merington, op. cit., pp. 265-66. This is a letter from Custer to Elizabeth, dated September 1873, from Camp in Montana Territory.

[25] Merington, op. cit., p. 266. This is a letter from Custer to Elizabeth, dated 23 September 1873, from Fort Abraham Lincoln, Dakota Territory.

[26] Custer, George A., "Battling With the Sioux On The Yellowstone," *Galaxy Magazine*, July, 1876, pp. 91-92, reprinted in *By Valor & Arms Magazine*, October 1974, p. 5.

CAVALRY BITS
One of Seven Volumes

The Yellowstone Expedition of 1873

2nd Lt. Charles Braden, formal portrait taken while on frontier duty just prior to Yellowstone Expedition. From the U. S. Army Military History Institute.

The Yellowstone Expedition of 1873[1]

by Lieutenant Charles Braden[2]
U. S. Army, Retired

The spring of 1873 the government decided to send an expedition to guard the surveyors of the Northern Pacific Railroad in their efforts to locate the line west of the Missouri River. The road had been built as far as Bismarck, Dakota, now in North Dakota. Considerable resistance was expected from the Indians, so a large force was to be sent. The Seventh Cavalry, to which I belonged, was to form part of the command. The regiment was scattered throughout the South, where we had been since 1871, taking part in suppressing the "Ku-Klux" organization.[3]

Our troop (L) was at Jackson Barracks, Louisiana.[4] Lieutenant (now Commissary General) Weston[5] was the first lieutenant and I was the second lieutenant. The captain, Sheridan[6], was on his brother's staff, so Weston was in command of the troop. It was a fine body of men, nearly every man an old soldier, for the vacancies in the troop, when we reached New Orleans in December, 1872, were about all filled by men who had served one or more terms in other regiments in the South, and when discharged drifted to the city; having soon spent their money they were ready to enlist again. It was known that we were to go on the expedition, and the prospect of active service was the magnet which drew a number to our ranks.

We were to go on a steamboat as far as Cairo, Illinois.[7] We were ready about the middle of March, but our departure was delayed because there was much floating ice in the Mississippi above Memphis. We started on the evening of April 1st, 1873. The trip, lasting about a week, was comfortable and pleasant, but rather tedious. At Memphis, we took aboard several troops of the regiment which had come by rail from their stations in South Carolina.[8] At Cairo the entire regiment was to be collected. We were all there on the same day, but not together, for two troops (D and I) left in the morning for St. Paul, where they were to form a portion of the escort of the commission to locate the northern boundary of the United States. Major Turning,[9] of the Engineers, was, I believe, in charge of this commission. We arrived at Cairo in the afternoon of the day D and I Troops left.

At Cairo we took trains for Yankton, Dakota. Traveling in those days for men and horses was not as comfortable as it is now. The regiment, after the expedition's return in the fall, was to be stationed at Forts Lincoln[10] and Rice[11], the former nearly across the Missouri River from Bismarck, and the latter about twenty-five miles south. It was to be a change of station to another department, so all baggage, public and private, was taken along, and there was a great deal of it.

The trip to Yankton[12] from Cairo was uneventful. Upon arriving at Yankton we went into camp on a low plain about two miles from the city. The officers' wives, who accompanied their husbands, went, all but two, to the best hotel in the town. The exceptions were Mrs. Custer and Mrs. Calhoun (General Custer's sister). They occupied a vacant house about midway between town and camp.[13]

Most of the officers and men wore the thin clothing which they had used in the South, and no one anticipated the great change in the climate that came upon us. A few days after our arrival, a typical Dakota blizzard set in. It began snowing on a Saturday morning and did not let up until the following Thursday. The strong wind piled the snow into hugh drifts and filled every hollow. Sunday morning the scene was extremely desolate. Some of the tents had split open at the top and the inmates were covered with anywhere from a few inches to a foot of snow. I woke up before dawn and felt the heavy weight. Getting dressed the best way possible I waited for daylight. I picked some of my belongings out of the snow and put what I could find into my trunks and covered the trunks with a poncho. I then went out to look around. The snow was so blinding that it was impossible to see twenty feet. I found my way over to the first sergeant's tent. We went along the picket line, and found that many of the horses were over half-buried in the snow. What to do was the question. There was no one to give orders, for General Custer was not well,[14] and also could not get over to camp. Before long, the Governor of the Territory, General McCook,[15] and General Forsyth,[16] one of General Sheridan's aides, reached camp and told us to get over to town with our horses as soon as possible, and the best way we could, and to take possession of several large buildings which the quartermaster had had constructed, and also any vacant houses we could find, and to put the animals under shelter.

General McCook said the blizzard would probably continue several days, and that the horses would perish if left outdoors. Fortunately the wind was blowing in the direction of the town. We put no saddles on the horses; each man rode bareback and with the snaffle bit. No semblance of order was possible, each trooper getting along as well as he could. Lieutenant Weston was away, and I was in command of the troop. I was the first to receive General McCook's directions. Every little while a rider would be thrown. There was no time to stop and help him, but he, had to look out for himself. After great exertions, we finally got the horses under shelter, and then we had to look out for a place for ourselves, as it was impossible to face the storm and go back to camp. Some of us found refuge in the town hotels; others were cared for by citizens in their homes. There were many laundresses and children in camp, and we became very anxious about them. Fortunately, the weather was not very cold, so they were in no immediate danger of freezing to death,[17] but we knew they must be suffering from hunger. On the third day of the storm several officers with a number of men endeavored to reach camp, but we were unable to face the driving wind and snow.

On the fifth day we succeeded, after several hours of the hardest work, in reaching camp. We found some of the women and children buried in the snow, a number had frostbitten hands and feet, and all of them were half dead with fright and lack of sustenance. They were put into sleds and dragged to town, where the kind-hearted citizens turned out en masse to aid the unfortunates in every way possible.[18]

After the storm was over we went back to camp with our horses. They were a sorry looking lot, all gaunt from hunger and thirst, and many without manes and tails, which had been knawed (sic) off by other animals in efforts to obtain a little nourishment. In a day or two the snow melted and our camp was, for several days, one vast lake.

Mrs. Custer, in "Boots and Saddles," describes this storm, but her account falls far short of a complete presentation of sufferings of those who were in the camp.[19]

After the ground became dry, we had an animated camp. It was the first time since the Wichita campaign of 1868[20] that as many as ten troops had been together. There were squad drills, company drills, squadron drills and regimental drills daily, ending every evening with a dress parade mounted. To witness this came the people of the surrounding country for miles. Entertainments by citizens of Yankton were given several times each week. With few exceptions the married officers had their families with them. Time passed rapidly and pleasantly, while we were getting ready for the long march to Fort Rice, where the main body of the "Yellowstone expedition" of 1873 was to rendezvous.

General Stanley,[21] colonel of the Twenty-second Infantry, was in command. I have forgotten the exact composition of the expedition,[22] but there were about all the companies of the Twenty-second Infantry, six companies of the Ninth Infantry, four of the Eighth Infantry, and one or two of the Sixth Infantry, several of the Seventh Infantry, besides a detachment of Ree Indians under Lieutenant Daniel Brush,[23] Seventeenth Infantry. There was an immense wagon train, for supplies had to be carried for the long march to Glendive,[24] on the Yellowstone River, where we were to meet some steamboats with additional supplies for the trip west along the Yellowstone.

In moving up the Missouri from Yankton each troop was allowed two wagons, enough to carry a few days' rations for the men and forage for the horses. A flat-bottom steamboat went along loaded with supplies. Of course, our march was across the bends of the river, while the steamer had to follow the windings, and probably went at least twice as far, if not more, every day than we did. The families of the officers, excepting Mrs. Custer and Mrs. Calhoun, were on the boat. Several times each week. the camp was almost alongside the steamer. The passengers on the boat found it a very monotonous trip, their only consolation being that they were always sheltered from the heavy rainstorms to which we were exposed.

I was caterer of our mess on the march from Yankton to Fort Rice. In the mess were Colonel Benteen,[25] Dr. Kimball,[26] Lieutenants Weston, Gibson,[27] DeRudio[28] and myself. Before leaving Yankton I purchased enough eggs to fill two barrels. These eggs were carefully packed in oats, and the last of them were not used till after we reached Fort Rice. They were a welcome addition to our bill of fare. Our cook was a colored woman called "Sam" — abbreviation for Samuella.[29]

One interesting incident, perhaps worth describing, occurred during the march. One night our camp was pitched near an Indian village. We noticed that there were no young men, all the Indians being old, worn-out warriors, women and children. The absence of the young bucks was due to the fact that they were on the war-path, and we afterwards met them in several affairs. The villagers soon visited our camp and made themselves at home. When our mess was about finishing dinner, which was served on a large box, we sitting around on smaller boxes or camp stools, five squaws (one old and the others from about sixteen to twenty years old) came near. Dr. Kimball had served in the Sioux country and knew a little of the language. He asked them to come nearer, and they sat on the ground. Our dinner consisted of roast beef, mashed potatoes, canned tomatoes and hot biscuits, baked in a "Dutch oven."

When we had finished we gave each squaw a piece of beef and some vegetables, with a knife and a fork. They had evidently never seen a fork, and did not know what to do with it. After a minute's talk among themselves they laid the forks behind them on the ground and used their fingers to carry the food to their mouths. When nothing more could be gathered with their fingers they used their tongues and literally "licked the platters clean." All the while they curiously eyed our colored Sam, who returned their stares, expressing at the same time in language more forcible than elegant, her opinion of the squaws.

The latter, evidently beholding a negress for the first time,[30] seemed to be much interested in her looks, although they said nothing that we understood. As the last course to the dinner, each of the squaws was given a hot biscuit, inside of which had been placed a lump of butter. At first they were suspicious that some trick was about to be played on them (they had undoubtedly never seen hot bread) but as we ate biscuits prepared as were those given to them, their courage came back, and having tasted one the biscuits could not be buttered rapidly enough. On the whole it was a unique dinner party. We learned that the squaws were Mrs. Two Bears and the four Misses Two Bears.[31]

At Fort Rice the department commander, General Alfred Terry,[32] visited our camp, reviewed and inspected the regiment. Afterwards a reception was given him at the quarters of the commanding officer.

When everything was ready, the expedition started on its long journey. Whenever the circumstances were favorable the wagon train was in four columns. Half of the infantry marched in front and half in the rear of the train. The cavalry was equally divided into left and right wings, and marched on the flanks of the train.

It was not known how long it would require to reach Glendive, and it was necessary to take as many stores as possible, so officers were restricted in what they could take. Mess chests, cots and trunks were prohibited. Each officer could take a valise with a change of underclothing, roll of blankets, and each mess a few cooking utensils. An inspection was made to see that no officer exceeded the allowance, but one managed to take his mess chest and a cooking stove. The cook stove came to grief before long, due to a few peculiar circumstances.

Before the expedition was well under way a poker club had been started in the cavalry camp. One of the rules was that play must stop at midnight. Reveille was at 3, breakfast at 4, and advance at 5 every morning. One morning the poker players were late at breakfast, and when the advance was sounded the cooking outfit with the stove was not ready to move on time. I was officer of the guard, and received directions to stay behind till this outfit was loaded, and then see that it caught up with its proper place in the column.

Soon, General Stanley rode up and asked what we were doing there and why we were not where we should be. The excuse of the soldier in charge of the mess was that the breakfast was late and the stove was too hot to handle. General Stanley said a few emphatic words about officers having stoves in violation of orders, and declared that the stove should not again delay the entire command. The next day there was no stove in camp, and I presume the pieces of it are still rusting somewhere in Dakota.

There had been heavy rains and the ground was quite soft. Progress was very slow, for the wagons had heavy loads. In about two weeks we did not go fifty miles, and it was decided to send all empty wagons back to Fort Lincoln for extra supplies of rations and forage. Our squadron, under Captain Yates,[33] was detailed as escort. The return trip was quite rapid, as our train was light. We had to wait several days at Lincoln before we could get enough to fill our wagons. We had heard of the mosquitoes along the Missouri River bottom, but never dreamed that the pests could be so numerous and so troublesome. After our experience I was ready to believe any mosquito story that could be told, even to that I afterwards heard my West Point roommate tell.[34] After graduation he served awhile in Alaska and declared that the mosquitoes there were so large and strong that each carried under his wing a small whetstone on which to sharpen his bill. Another of his stories was to the effect that netting was no protection, for the "skeeters" always get through. He had seen them do it, saying that they worked in threes, and when they encountered a net two stuck their bills into an opening and pulled the mesh apart so that the third could go through. Then this one pulled one way from the inside, one pulled the other way from the outside, and the second one went through. Then the two inside pulled and the last one entered. When they had feasted to their heart's content they simply reversed the process of entering, and went out.

After getting our wagons loaded at Lincoln we started after the main command, but did not overtake it until we reached Glendive. Our trip to Glendive was made as rapidly as possible. We followed the trail of the main command and had the benefit of their roadmaking, so that there was no delay to us. Our marches were long, for we endeavored to make daily double the distance gone by General Stanley. Our camping places at night were at every other camp of the main force. There were no exciting incidents on this march, but we passed through a part of the famous "Bad Lands" of Dakota and Montana.

At Glendive was the steamer *Josephine*,[35] loaded with supplies. There was great activity in camp. A small earthwork was constructed, and all the suppplies that could not be loaded into wagons were to be left with a guard under Captain Pearson,[36] Seventeenth Infantry, to await the return of the expedition after the summer's work was finished.

Some days after our arrival at Glendive, the expedition pulled out for the really difficult part of the journey. We had to pass over some more of the "Bad Lands," and after several days of toilsome and very slow marching we got clear of them near the mouth of the Powder River. At this place we were again met by the *Josephine*, which brought us the last mail we had until the return in September. In looking over a New York paper I saw a notice of a disastrous fire in my native city of East Saginaw, Michigan. My father's house was burned in this fire.

We fully expected to meet Indians, and orders were given to be on the lookout for signs. As day after day passed and none were seen, the men became careless and there was considerable straggling while looking for water. The line of march was along the north bank of the Yellowstone, but every morning the wagon train took to the high lands, and cut across the bends. General Custer with two troops of cavalry went ahead each day in order to look out for the best route for the train.[37] The troops took turns for this duty, which was far more agreeable than to go with the train. As frequently happened, when ravines or creeks were to be crossed, the wagons had to go singly, and it took hours to get them over. In such cases there was a tedious wait, and the horses were unbridled and permitted to graze if any grass was to be found.

The engineers of the railroad surveyed their route along the river's bank. As they were separated from us, an escort of a company of infantry and a troop of cavalry was every day assigned for their protection. There were, after the two details for Custer's advance guard and the engineers' escort, but five cavalry troops left for the two flanks of the wagon train, three on one side and two on the other.

One day during a halt some of the officers thought they saw a few Indians several miles ahead. They supposed the Indians were lying among some rocks. I was the only officer of the regiment who carried a field glass. Everyone present took a turn with the glasses. There were as many opinions as there were lookers. Finally Bloody Knife,[38] the scout and guide, appeared; shading his eyes with his hands he took a long look, and said there were no Indians. Then using the glass, he confirmed his first ideas, and said that what we saw was a piece of half burned log and a few rocks. An hour later we passed the place. Bloody Knife was correct. His naked eyes were better than ours with the glasses thrown in.

On the 4th of August we were opposite the mouth of Tongue River. It was the hottest day we had had. Custer had as usual gone ahead with Troops A and B. Troop F was part of the escort of the surveyors. Our troop (L) was the rear of the left flank, between the train and the rear. About 2 o'clock in the afternoon the train came to a stop, at a place where it was necessary for the wagons to go one by one over a gully. Long before this, scores of infantrymen had succumbed to the heat, and crawled into the wagons. The horses would not graze; they stood motionless with their heads lowered and the tongues protruding. We sat in the shade made by the bodies of the animals, and found a little relief from the broiling sun. The air was a dead calm, and we afterwards heard that one of the hospital attendants said the thermometer on the shady side of an ambulance had registered 110°. The officers and men were about as languid as the horses.

Suddenly the scene was changed. A few shots were heard to our left and rear. Although we had not seen up to this time any Indians or signs of them, we felt that the shots meant something doing. Everyone jumped up and quickly put the bridle on his horse. At this time the column moved forward, and in another minute we saw coming toward us, as fast as he could urge his horse, a single rider, behind him his picket pin flying up and down as it struck some obstruction. As he approached us Weston and I rode out to meet him. As he got within hearing he yelled, "All down there are killed."[39]

He belonged to F Troop, which was a part of the engineer escort. We at once concluded that the engineers and their escort had been attacked and that this man had escaped from the supposed slaughter. Such, however, was not the case. The soldier with another had straggled and looked for water. They had joined the veterinary surgeon of the regiment and the post trader. The four finding a spring had taken the bridles off their horses, picketed them out to graze, and were sitting near the spring, when they were surprised by a small party of Indians. The two civilians fell at the first round, but the soldiers pulled up the picket pins and started to get away. They were pursued, and one was killed, the other escaping unhurt and giving us warning.[40]

Lieutenant Weston at once sent word ahead to the officer in command of our wing, and gave orders for the men to go in the direction of the firing. We were on a very high plateau, probably three hundred feet above the river. The descent was very steep and covered with loose stones of all sizes. The men scattered, each going down as best he could, with orders to assemble at the bottom of the hill. I was fortunate in finding the best place for the descent — it was in a little valley — and was the first to get down. The horses were led, and at times fairly slid on their haunches. Loose stones, started above us, came whirling past our heads, and it is a wonder that no one was injured. A few of the men were close behind me.

A minute or so before we reached the bottom, and travelling at right angles to our direction, rode at a trot five or six Indians, leading several horses, one of which I recognized as that of our veterinary surgeon, because of the size of the animal, and the red saddle blanket. We could easily have fired on and probably killed some of the party, but we thought they belonged to the Ree scouts with us. They were in fact, as we afterwards learned, Rain-in-the-Face[41] and a few of his warriors who had killed, as before mentioned, the veterinary and trader and appropriated their horses and other belongings.

In a few minutes more the entire troop was down the hill and assembled. Saddle girths were tightened and we moved up the valley of the Yellowstone. Ahead of us was Rain-in-the-Face and party going as fast as they could. We then realized that the Indians were hostiles, and we started in pursuit.

After going probably a mile we rounded the point of a bluff. A glance up the valley showed that the grass had been set on fire. It was in patches, large and small, and being quite dry, burned readily. Soon we were riding between these burning patches, occasionally dashing across one. It was not possible to keep the men together. For probably half an hour we were in this situation. Between the heat of the sun and that of the burning grass it is inconceivable how we escaped loss; but all finally were through the fire.

A stop was made to collect the scattered troopers, and while waiting I used my glasses to survey the land. Way up the river was more smoke, and as it cleared away we could see many mounted men riding to and fro. Again the saddles were adjusted, each man loaded his carbine, and in line we moved on. Not long afterwards a mounted man rode out of a clump of woods and came in our direction. He was one of Custer's party. Custer had in the morning marched rapidly and soon was farther in advance than it was possible for the wagon train to go. Then he stopped in a small grove of cottonwood trees. The horses were unsaddled and picketed out to graze, and most of the men went to sleep. Along in the afternoon, about the time our stragglers were attacked, a large number of Indians attacked Custer's party.

From what we could learn of the affair it came near being a surprise to Custer, but fortunately the Indians were discovered just in time. While some of the men formed a skirmish line to stand off the warriors, the others brought in the horses. Custer was comparatively safe in the grove so long as his ammunition held out. The Indians, foiled in their attempt to surprise the command and to stampede the horses, set fire to the grass, and hoped to burn out the besieged troopers, but the grass in the woods was not very dry and did not burn rapidly, so this plan was a failure. It was this fire which, spreading down the valley, caught us in its warm embrace. I have never been in such a hot situation, and I hope I may never again be either in this world or in the next.

We had distanced the balance of the left wing. If they started up the valley they must have gotten lost, for we did not see them again until night. Our approach caused the Indians attacking Custer to withdraw. When we were near enough to Custer's position to be distinguished from hostile Indians, Custer is said to have remarked, "Ten to one that is Weston and his troop in the lead." "A safe bet, General," said Major Moylan, "but there are no takers." This remark, surely a great compliment to Weston and L Troop, was well deserved.

When we halted there was not a man who did not look as black as the ace of spades; the smoke of the burning grass had stuck to our faces; all had perspired so much that we were as wet as if we had been in the river. Perspiration was dripping from the horses and many a leg was badly singed while galloping through the patches of burning grass. I crawled on all fours far enough into the Yellowstone to get my head under water. It felt as if ice had been packed around me. The water itself was not so very cold, but it felt so in our overheated condition.

After waiting several hours, and there being no indications of the wagon train, Custer retraced his steps and near sundown met the wagons. The veterinary surgeon and post trader, as well as one trooper, were missing. Searching parties were sent out and the bodies of the two former were found, but not that of the soldier. They were covered with canvas and carried along next day. Their burial was mentioned in the October, 1904, number of the *Cavalry Journal*. A month later, then the expedition was on its return, a skeleton was found near where the veterinary and trader had been killed. This was probably the missing soldier.

After this day's experience there was no more straggling, and everyone was on the alert to discover signs of Indians. We were now in the vicinity of a number of villages. On the 5th, 6th and 7th we passed several places where there had been large camps, and also noted heavy trains coming from the north. On the 8th a number of large campsites were passed, in some of which were abandoned articles of value to the Indians. It was reported that a rifle had also been found. Less than twenty-four hours had elapsed since some of these camps had been used. On the afternoon of August 8th, General Stanley directed Custer to take every mounted man, including the Ree Indians, make a forced march and endeavor to *overtake the villages*. About three days' rations were carried on pack animals. A blanket and overcoat was allowed each man — soldiers and officers — and about one hundred rounds per man of extra ammunition were taken. No tents were permitted, not even for the commanding officer. An extra feed of grain was given to the horses, and we started as soon as it became dark, and with brief halts marched all night. At sunrise we stopped an hours to graze the horses and let the men get some breakfast. All day of the 9th we moved as rapidly as we could, being stimulated by fresh signs, and hoped to overtake the village we were following. On the evening of this day we reached the place on the Yellowstone where the Indians had crossed the river. They had probably taken their belongings over in "bull boats" and made their ponies swim. The boats were made by stretching hides over a wicker frame work, and; it required skillful navigating to keep them from upsetting.

On the march during this day we noticed where large accessions to the Indian villages had been made, by the number of heavy trails which joined the main party. By evening the command was tired out. We had been on the go all day and night of the 8th and all day of the 9th —thirty-six hours — with very brief halts. Till darkness set in efforts were made to find a ford, but without success. We bivouacked where we were, and by the next morning we were very much refreshed.

Next day, the 10th, at sunrise parties were sent up and down the river to look for a crossing.[42] The main force went to a small island. Someone had discovered a narrow ford to the island capable of holding two or three abreast; but between the island and the south bank the water was deep and the current strong. Efforts were made to swim some of the horses across, their riders to carry a rope made by tying a lot of picket lines together. The efforts failed, for the long line was too heavy to be dragged through the water with its strong current. Lieutenant Weston and several teamsters succeeded in crossing with mules.

Our men and horses had never been drilled in swimming. When the water reached about halfway between their bellies and their backs the strong current nearly carried them off their feet, and the animals refused to go further, but turned around and started for the shore. The swimmers were advised to keep on their underclothing, but they did not do so, and long before the day was over the sun had blistered their bodies, and the next morning they were stiff and sore all over. The men who swam across explored the woods and found many indications that the Indians had been there but a short time before. It was afterwards stated that a few redskins were concealed in the bushes and watched our efforts. They might have killed those of our command who crossed, for the latter were stark naked and without any means of defense. Their danger was very great, for a single armed Indian could easily have killed them all without any risk of injury to himself.

The entire command remained huddled on the little island until night, when it returned to the north bank of the river and went into bivouac. It was decided to move up the river the next day and seek a crossing, but the Indians themselves solved the problem by coming back after getting their village to a place of safety.

The bivouac of L Troop was farthest upstream. It was my turn for officer of the guard that night. Pickets were posted on the bluffs, and some hours after dark all except the sentinels endeavored to obtain a little sleep. About 2 o'clock next morning I felt sure I heard sounds that resembled those made by horses running over hard ground. I thought that some of our animals had become stampeded; but one of our scouts said that the sounds we heard were made by ponies, and that the Indians were undoubtedly concentrating in the woods opposite us, and would open fire at daybreak. The scout thought that General Custer ought to be notified. I followed his advice, and went to where General Custer was asleep, woke him up, and told him what the scout had said. Custer replied that he did not believe the Indians were coming back. His manner indicated that he was annoyed at being awakened. I was also annoyed at the manner of my early reception, and went back to the guard.

The pony sounds continued, and the scout declared that by daylight there would be several hundred warriors in the woods opposite, and that they would make it warm for us, as we had no protection whatever except a few scattered trees, and the width of the river was less then the range of their Henry rifles. It turned out as the scout had predicted.

As the mist on the river became dissipated by the rising

sun, a hot fire was opened upon us. The cooks, preparing coffee, were the only ones astir, and, for all but the scout and myself, it was a complete surprise. The bottom on which we were bivouacked was about half a mile broad, and orders were given to move back out of range. A number of skirmishes were scattered along the bank of the river and returned the fire of the Indians. I had gone to where Keegan, the cook of our mess, was preparing coffee for Weston and myself. The bullets were flying around at a lively rate. I called to Keegan[43] to take the coffeepot along. Just as he stooped to take it from the fire several bullets struck the blaze and some of the live coals fell on his hand. The result was that he dropped the pot, our precious coffee was spilled, and all we had for breakfast was hard-tack and water.

One of the horses of the guard had been left behind when we moved out of range. With one of the troopers I went back to get the animal and had barely pulled up the picket pin when the animal leaped into the air and fell dead, a bullet from the other side having gone through his brain. I next went to a high bluff from which could be seen the country for eight or ten miles up and down the river. With the aid of my glasses I was able to notice that numbers of Indians were crossing and approaching our position from both directions. A report of this was at once sent to General Custer and he made his disposition accordingly. To the west were hills, which in possession of the hostiles would render our position in the bottom a very unsafe one. Our squadron commander was directed to occupy this hill with about a third of a troop, dismounted. I was ordered to turn over the guard to the sergeant and go in charge of this detachment. We went as rapidly as possible. and leaving our horses at the foot of the hill scrambled to the top through a narrow ravine. There were about twenty men with me.

As our party reached the top, spread out before us was a plateau probably a mile or more in extent and not a hundred yards away. Riding in our direction was what looked like the whole Sioux Nation to the few of us. There were probably a hundred dressed in their war toggery of paint, feathers, horns, etc. We saw them before they saw us, and hurriedly forming a line opened fire. One volley caused them to stop; several ponies were seen to fall, but I do not know if any of the warriors were hit. At any rate we saw several ponies an instant after scurrying back with two riders each. Our one volley caused them to turn, some to the right and some to the left, but close behind them was another lot of about the same number. Our men had barely time to slip a fresh cartridge into their carbines when the second line was where the first was checked. The second onslaught turned out as did the first. Our men were lying down on the slope, with only their heads above the summit. The fourth charge of the Indians came closer than any of the others, and to me it seemed as if some of them had gotten between us and the river, and would work to our rear. I arose and started to the left to see if this was the case, and had taken but a few steps, my right side toward the hostiles, when a bullet hit my left leg midway between the hip and the knee, and just missing the femoral artery, went clear through the leg, badly shattering the bone. I fell on my left side and rolled down the hill quite a distance. This put me out of business,[44] and I told the sergeant (Hall)[45] to take charge of the detachment. Hall was an old soldier and a very capable one.

As soon as the firing on us was heard in the valley below, the balance of our squadron, under Captain Yates, hurried to our relief, and upon their appearance the Indians withdrew. They were pursued up the valley a distance, but were not overtaken, as their ponies were in a much better condition than were our horses. Not one of the men with me was hit, but three or four had holes in their hats, and one had his hat-rim shot away.

While we were having our little fight there were more things doing in another part of the field. A party of Indians, who had crossed below us, moved forward and were met by Captain French.[46] In the fight that ensued several of the Indians were seen to fall, but were carried off the field by their comrades. Another party of warriors attacked the center of our position. They were driven off by Captain Tom Custer.[47] In this affair Lieutenant Ketcham, [48] Twenty-second Infantry, the assistant adjutant general of the expedition, had his horse shot under him. Custer's horse was also shot in this affair.

The pursuit continued about eight miles up the valley, where the Indians again crossed the river at the place where they had come over in the morning.

When the charge of the main body of our men was about to begin, the band was lined up and the regimental favorite, "Garryowen," struck up as an inspiration to the troopers.

The loss of the Indians in this affair is not known, but as they did the attacking, and exposed themselves freely, probably they had quite a number killed and wounded. Our loss, as reported by General Custer, was "one officer badly wounded, four men killed and three wounded; four horses killed and four wounded."

After the fighting on our side of the river was over, the hostiles again concentrated in the woods opposite us. Near sunset General Stanley arrived; with him were two pieces of artillery, three-inch rifles I believe. A few shells thrown across the river caused the Indians to abandon the woods.[49]

After this day we saw no more Indians, except a few who fired into our camp near what is called "Pompey's Pillar." They caused a little commotion among the men who were bathing or washing their clothes in the river.[50]

I recall an interesting experience of that summer. One day we were marching along in the bottom land, the officers to one side in order to avoid the dust, when, without warning, my horse went down and I was thrown over his head. It seemed as if the earth had opened under us. We had gotten into a quicksand hole or pit of unknown depth. Luckily it was not more than eight or nine feet across. Horse and rider floundered around and I felt myself going down. A picket line was thrown to me and I was pulled out, but a very sorry looking sight — mud and sand all over from the neck to the feet. The horse was also, after much difficulty, pulled out. My ride the balance of the day was anything but pleasant. The mud got dry, and my clothes became stiff. I suffered no injury from this experience, but lost one of my handsome spurs, which is way down somewhere in the bowels of the earth I suppose.

One afternoon, in camp, many of the men had washed their underclothing and put the articles on some low bushes to dry. A sudden whirlwind swept the camp and carried off a number of the garments. For a few minutes the air was full of them. Some lodged in the branches of cottonwood trees, and were with difficulty recovered; others when last seen were going heavenward, and they were never seen again by their owners. It was a ludicrous sight, but proved a serious thing to those who lost an only shirt, with no way of getting another till the return of the expedition.

On one occasion we had to cross a stream about forty feet or more wide, and too deep for fording. The banks were nearly perpendicular, and at least fifteen feet high. There were no trees anywhere around that were long enough to reach across. A unique bridge was constructed. Each wagon carried an extra tongue and reach, also a water keg holding about twenty gallons. Wagon bodies were filled with empty kegs. When enough to reach across — placed lengthwise in the stream — we so filled, they were put into the water, kegs underneath, and securely fastened with ropes. A row of stringers was laid on the upturned wagons, and on these a platform was constructed; all parts were lashed together as firmly as possible. The banks of the stream were dug away so that there was about a thirty degree slope on both sides. To test the bridge, some horses were led over, then some men rode over. The bridge did not sink more than a few inches under their weight, and was considered strong enough to bear a half-loaded wagon. The wagons were taken across by hand. Each was halted at the slope, the mules unhitched and driven across, where they were caught; the wheels were locked, and then the wagon pushed till it ran by itself. To the tongue was tied a rope with a hook at the loose end. Two men were at the tongue to guide the wagon, and two others carried the loose end of the rope. At the other side were two harnessed mules and a score of men.

As the wagon was pushed down the slope it gathered considerable speed. At the beginning of the bridge were two teamsters with spades. As the wagon passed them each with much skill and dexterity hit the lock with the edge of the spade. One stroke by each was generally sufficient to open the lock. As the wagon shot across the bridge the hook on the loose end of the rope was inserted into the ring on the whiffletree, the mules were shipped up and aided by men at the drag rope, the wagon was over and up the bank in less time than it takes to tell of it. The men with the spades rarely missed the first trial at unlocking. At first, the ambulances and light wagons were tried, but it was soon seen that the bridge was strong and would stand more strain. When the heavily loaded vehicles went on the bridge it sank below the surface, but readily arose as soon as the weight came off. Everything worked smoothly and well; there was not a breakdown and our entire command crossed without an accident. It was an interesting sight to witness. It required less than a minute to cross each wagon. I believe the bridge was designed and constructed by Lieutenant P. H. Ray,[51] Eighth Infantry.

While we were at Lincoln I had the good fortune to witness a "scalp dance" by the Ree Indians. In a skirmish, a short time previous to our arrival, the Sioux had lost one of their number, whose body fell into the hands of the Rees. He was, of course, scalped. It is not possible for me to describe the ceremony as it was enacted there on the plains amid the great surrounding stillness an hour or so after sunset. Yet in memory it cannot be quite forgotten.

In a circle were the Indian women, young girls and boys. The warriors, between thirty and forty in number, were gorgeous in all their war paint and feathers, and they formed an inner circle, in the center of which was an old squaw holding aloft on a long pole the scalp. The warriors were formed one behind the other and so close together that no one could pass between any two. They slowly moved around the old squaw with the scalp and kept up a continual chant, every few minutes giving vent to piercing whoops, at the expiration of which the squaw, in her turn, violently shook the pole and gave a few wild screeches. Occasionally one of the warriors in the ring turned his face toward us, gave a sardonic grin, shook his fist at the scalp and yelled, "Sioux, damn _____." (in language not to be printed), and which evidently was the extent of his English vocabulary.

The chanting of the braves had for its accompaniment the incessant noise of tin kettles and pans, beaten by the squaws and children. Fires were kept going, and it seemed to us as we stood there, watching through the smoke the moving figures with their painted faces and listening to the unceasing noise of their kettles as it came to our ears, that we had been suddenly transported to a scene from the infernal regions.

One brave who had been shot in the fight when the scalp was taken, was the hero of the occasion. He was mounted on a box near by and attended by several squaws, and proudly exhibited a severe flesh wound.

I saw this ceremony for two evenings, with no apparent change of the program noticeable to us. On the morning after the last dance the scalp was, with great ceremony, escorted to a steamer going up the river, and taken to the headquarters of the tribe at Fort Berthold, [52] where it was placed with their other trophies.

The Rees were, before the dances, in mourning for the loss of one of their braves killed sometime before in a fight

with the Sioux Indians, and the period of their mourning was to continue till a Sioux scalp could be taken in battle and certain ceremonies took place.

Another interesting incident at Lincoln was the case of a sick Indian for whom the post surgeon prescribed. He became worse, much to the surgeon's surprise, and it was hinted that the surgeon's prescription was disregarded, and the "medicine man" was treating the suffering warrior. An investigation brought out the fact that the drugs prescribed by the surgeon had never been taken, but that the "medicine man" had forced a nail under the skin just behind the ear. This had caused a festered sore. The nail was removed and the invalid rapidly recovered.

Before the expedition left Fort Rice a "medical survey" was held and some enlisted men and two officers were found physically unfit to undertake the hardships of the summer's campaign. One of the officers was a peculiar character. He was a very intelligent man, well educated. Before the Rebellion he had been Judge of a Federal Court in one of the Territories and a member of Congress. He was left at Rice in command of the camp of laundresses and such enlisted men as were not permitted to go with the expedition. [53] He started a small farm. His crops were growing nicely and promised a big harvest, when a countless number of grasshoppers appeared and everything in sight was devoured by the pests. Following the hoppers came flocks of blackbirds that became fat on a grasshopper diet. Then a happy idea came to Colonel _____. He procured a shotgun, gathered in as many of the birds as he wanted and made potpies of them. He afterwards said: "The _____ hoppers came along, by _____, and ate my garden, by _____, then the birds ate the hoppers, by _____, and we killed and ate the birds, by _____; so that we were even in the long run, by _____." The reader may put in the proper expletives.

I recall a hail storm narrative, told by an officer of the Sixth Infantry.[54] His company did not join the main command at Fort Rice, but was to meet it a few marches out. The company was caught in a hail storm. It was a typical Western storm, differing from the traditional storms in that the stones were about the size of ostrich eggs instead of hen's eggs. The men were stampeded, and ran for a bluff near by. The first to reach it put their heads into any small hole that was convenient, their bodies, of course, protruding and receiving a severe pelting. As others reached the bluff, the larger and stronger fellows pulled their weaker brethren from their holes and stuck their own heads in. The officer said it was a ludicrous sight.

I have written the above from memory, after a lapse of thirty-two years. There may be a few slight errors, but if so, they are trivial. I had kept a diary, in which was entered every night the length of our march, time of going into camp, nature of the country passed over during the day, if good grass, wood and water were found, and whatever incidents of the day I thought would be of interest later on. After I was wounded nearly everyone thought I could not possibly survive the long journey ahead. My effects became scattered and the note book was lost, together with my saber and remaining spur.[55]

Footnotes

[1] This article first appeared in the *Cavalry Journal,* October, 1905.

[2] Charles Braden was born on 23 November 1847, in Detroit, Michigan. His interests in all things military, and in serving his country in particular, were focused as early as the beginning of the Civil War when, after the guns of Sumter resounded throughout the land, young Charles Braden, age 13 and some months, carrying a heavy musket, walked many long miles to a recruiting station. His patriotic gesture, though appreciated, was not honored. The desire to wear the uniform of his country was realized when he received an appointment to the United States Military Academy in 1865; he graduated in June, 1869, 19th in a class of 39, Cullum #2291.

Upon graduation he was assigned as a Second Lieutenant in the 7th U. S. Cavalry, serving first on the frontier, and then "reconstruction duty" in Louisiana and South Carolina. This disagreeable duty was to be relieved by another frontier assignment in 1873, when the 7th Cavalry was assigned the duty of protecting the Northern Pacific Railroad survey teams who were seeking an extension route westward from Bismarck. This duty was to become known as the Yellowstone Expedition of 1873. Lieutenant Braden was seriously wounded in a skirmish with the Indians and as a result spent the balance of the expedition in a stretcher. He was carried in this litter for a total of twenty-eight days at which time the expedition reached the reserve camp at Glendive, Montana, and he was transferred to the steamer, *Josephine,* for the return trip to Fort Lincoln.

Because of the permanent incapacity his continuance on active service was deemed impossible, so in June, 1878, nine short years from West Point, he was placed on the retired list of the army. Though recommended for the Medal of Honor, "political rivalry" deprived him of this singular distinction.

After retirement he was most successful in conducting private schools at West Point, Cornwall-on-Hudson and Highland Falls, New York. One year after his retirement he married Jeanette, daughter of General Thomas Devin.

Charles Braden died peacefully at his home in Highland Falls, on January 15, 1919, and was interred in the West Point cemetery on the 17th of January.

William J. Roe, who, incidentally, was in the same graduating class with General Godfrey, wrote: "The Indian Wars are ended; Sitting Bull and Black Kettle and Geronimo and Satanta have gone to keep company on the 'happy hunting grounds' with Massasoit and Miantonomoh; but the romance and chivalry of the days of border war in the wild west can never pass. The stories of Washita and Wounded Knee and the Little Big Horn and the Yellowstone will be told in coming centuries, when perhaps a new civilization shall have banashed forever in-justice and brutality and organized murder." (*Annual Report,* United States Military Academy, June 10, 1919.)

[3] The entire 7th U. S. Cavalry had been "distributed" around the country, some in Louisiana, some in South Carolina and some in Kentucky. Suppressing the Ku Klux Klan was but part of their assignments; they also were buying horses for the cavalry and crushing the illicit "whiskey trade of the hills."

"When the 7th Cavalry was transferred from stations in Kansas in 1871 to stations in the South, we had the same station at Yorkville, South Carolina at the time of the Ku Klux Klan disturbances. We were frequently sent over on 'raids.' I secured the Constitution and By Laws of the Ku Klux Klan and was the first witness in the prosecution to identify that document to prove the conspiracy." (Godfrey to Roe, *Narrative.* p. 2.) This was but one example of the diversification of the 7th Cavalry's duties and an indication of the extent of their distribution. It took the Yellowstone Expedition of 1873 to bring them all back together once again.

[4] The first United States troops arrived in New Orleans on December 20, 1803, so that the city was garrisoned with the intention of guarding against slave insurrections. This was called the Post of New Orleans. In 1834, new barracks were erected on the left bank of the Mississippi below the city, originally called New Orleans Barracks, but after the Civil War was renamed Jackson Barracks. (Prucha, Francis Paul, *A Guide To The Military Posts of the United States,* p. 94) The buildings were constructed of brick and granite. The quarters for enlisted men consisted of four separate buildings, two stories high, **each 53 by 32 feet and surrounded by a spacious veranda, with an occupancy of about 45 men.** Officers' quarters were contained in seven two-story buildings, two of which measured 42 by 21 feet, and five 82 by 21 feet. The post was designed to accommodate four companies of infantry and a hospital. In addition to the hospital there were other buildings such as the dead-house, bakery, library, water reservoir, guardhouse, etc. The cavalry, when posted there, had their stables in an inclosure in the rear of the barracks. The one amusing fact was that there was no arrangement for bathing, either in

Yellowstone Expedition of 1874   69

summer or winter. Good swimmers could bathe after night in the river, but seemingly only in the summer. (Billings, John S., *Surgeon General's Report on Barracks and Hospitals, Circular #4*, pp. 162-165.)

There were no wash or bath rooms, and the men washed near the cisterns. There were two large sinks, built of brick, about 8 feet deep, sloping on all sides toward the bottom, and lined with cement; they were cleaned through a trap opening from the level of the ground into the sink. They were disinfected twice daily, were provided with two urinals each, and were good and convenient. River-water was supplied to the rooms, both up and down stairs, through pipes leading from the large tank in the tower and the southwest angle of the post. There was one cistern to each building. Water closets were situated in the yards; they were brick sinks, cleaned through a trap in the floor. (Billings, John S., *Surgeon General's Report on the Hygiene of the United States Army, Circular No. 8*, pp. 135-138) As could be expected, disease was common with fever and social diseases leading the list. There were no reports in either of the Circulars concerning health and hygiene for officers and their families. And although it was located in Louisiana, Jackson Barracks came under the jurisdiction of the Department of Texas. (Thian, Raphael P., *Notes Illustrating the Military Geography of the United States*, p. 99.)

[5] John Francis Weston of Kentucky who began his career on 24 December 1861 as a First Lieutenant in the 4th Kentucky Cavalry. As the text states, was Commissary General, being appointed that on 6 December 1900. He was also a recipient of the Medal of Honor, for gallantry at Wetumka, Alabama, during the Civil War. It was awarded on 9 April 1898. (Heitman, Francis B., *Historical Register And Dictionary of the United States Army*, p. 1021.)

[6] Michael Vincent Sheridan of Ohio who began his career on 7 September 1863, as a First Lieutenant in the 2nd Missouri Infantry. He held many brevets for gallantry in action and meritorious service during the Civil War. He was made Brigadier General, U.S.A. on 15 April 1902, and retired the next day. (Heitman, p. 881.)

[7] Cairo, Illinois and Peducah, Kentucky, were natural depots for the armies travelling east, west, north and south. Between the two cities, the great Mississippi and Ohio Rivers made natural highways. These two cities were often used as staging areas for travel.

[8] These regiments had been on the tedious duty of chasing the Ku Klux Klan and the illicit whiskey trade as previously stated. It represented the first time in years the regiment had been together, and old acquaintances were renewed.

[9] A search of all the military registers failed to disclose a Major Turning.

[10] This was Fort Abraham Lincoln established in 1872, and closed in 1891. In the beginning, 14 June 1872, it was nothing more than a

temporary camp named Fort McKeen and originally located on the west bank of the Missouri River near Bismarck, North Dakota. Its original purpose was to house the troops who were to protect the construction crews of the Northern Pacific Railroad. It was serving this purpose in 1873. In August of 1872, the post was moved about five miles from its original site, and on 19 November 1872, it was named Fort Abraham Lincoln. It was closed on 22 July 1891. (Prucha, p. 55.)

[11] Fort Rice was established on 7 July 1864, by General Alfred Sully, and its original purpose was to be a supply base for the military operations against the Sioux. It was located on the right bank of the Missouri River, about 10 miles north of the mouth of the Cannonball River. It was closed on 25 November 1878. (Prucha, p. 102.)

[12] Yankton, Dakota Territory (South Dakota) was settled in 1858 and was the capital of Dakota Territory from 1861 to 1883. It is located on the Missouri River 60 miles southwest of present day Sioux Falls, and then as now was a railroad center. (Websters *Geographical Dictionary*, p. 1279.)

Godfrey's succinct narrative of the trip from Yankton makes good reading and is very revealing about the life of a soldier in the field, especially on a half-civilized frontier. It is also particularly revealing when personalities are discussed: "We left Yankton early in May and were a month marching the 500 miles up the Missouri valley to Fort Rice, 25 miles below Bismarck, Dakota, where were assembled the trips for 'Stanley's Yellowstone Expedition.' The march up the valley was, regimentally considered, an eventful one. For two years, in the Southern States, the troops had been scattered, usually one troop to a station. The officers, generally, had successfully managed their local duties and endeavored to avoid friction with the whites, whose political aim was to free their states from 'Negro domination.' So when the troops assembled at Memphis and Cairo there was, in addition to the joy of reunion of comrades, a spirit of self satisfaction and independence, that denoted the mood of unity, discipline. Gen. Custer in matters of discipline gave little or no attention to the enlisted men. He held his officers responsible. Unfortunately he put all officers. high, low, old and [molded them in] the form of our C. O., General Custer. Formal greetings, a few common-place remarks, silence. I tried to hitch up some team converation but of rather doubtful success. I gave the General a 'box seat' (ordinary packing box for canned goods!). Invariably my former guests would knock their pipes against their boot heel, yawn two or three times and drowsily announce 'well, it's my bed time, good night,' or, 'I'm pretty tired tonight, so I'll say good night,' etc. — until we were left to ourselves. He declined to take my only folding chair, vacated by one of my former guests, saying he preferred his box seat. We talked about the War (Civil War), of the Generals, their characteristics, abilities, mistakes, successes, etc., but dwelt more particularly on

West Point reminiscences — but never one word about the regiment or our officers. Thus time passed until after midnight. Our conversations had been rather unrestrained but always serious, seldom a laugh and rarely a smile . . . and rarely holding to individual accountability. In individual cases on this march he would place the officer in arrest, and then issue a 'circular' to the whole command indicating that the direction was general and not individual. Those who sympathized with his principal aim, discipline, were at first dumbfounded, and then outraged; some days two or three 'circulars' would be issued. (You see, copies of GOs & SOs were sent to Dept. Hdqrs. but 'circulars' were not!) It was exasperating and then besides he denied privileges, such as going to the supply steamer on the river near camp, on board which were our families. It got so that outside of family, general, 'cut' Hqrs, where Mrs. Custer & Mrs. Calhoun (his sister) were in the evenings.

"One evening, chill and misty, I had quite a bonfire of drift-wood in front of my tent, and after supper several officers came to have their evening smoke and 'swap lies.' In the midst of our cheer, out of the darkness . . . he looked at his watch, snapped it shut, said good night, and shot off with the misty gloom towards his Hqrs. I went to bed — and then reveille at 4 a.m.!

"Braden and I were together nearly every day, always chummy. He was fortunate in his Troop Commanders, Lt. John F. Weston, afterwards . . . Major General U. S. A. They were congenial and happy dispositions and ever afterward maintained a warm friendship." (Godfrey to Roe, pp. 7-9.)

This portion of Godfrey's narrative seems neither to praise or condemn Custer, but rather projects puzzlement over his behavior. It may have been the broodings which culminated in the famous Custer-Stanley feud. It could be many things, but Godfrey, inconsistent with his later years and writings, offered no explanation.

[13] Elizabeth described their shelter thusly: ". . . some of the kind-hearted soldiers found the owner in a distant cabin, and he rented it to us for several days. The place was equal to a palace to me. There was no plastering, and the house seemed hardly weather-proof. It had a floor, however, and an upper story divided off by beams; over these Mary [Calhoun] and I stretched blankets and shawls and so made two rooms." (Custer, Elizabeth, *Boots and Saddles*, p. 19.)

[14] The General had indeed become very ill. Braden's passing remark hardly signifies the depth and extent of his illness. Elizabeth explained: "Without his knowledge, I sent for the surgeon, who, like all of his profession in the army, came promptly. He gave me some powerful medicine to administer every hour, and forbade the general to leave his bed . . . The general was too ill for me to venture to find my usual comfort from his re-assuring voice . . . I grew more and more terrified at our utterly desolate condition and his continued

illness, though fortunately he did not suffer. He was too ill, and I too anxious..." (Custer, Elizabeth, op. cit., pp. 19-25.) Elizabeth went on to explain how the soldiers suffered even though the townspeople had made fruitless efforts to alleviate the suffering from the cold. Eventually the blizzard subsided, everyone got food, and health was slowly returned to the seriously ill. But the General's illness deserved more than just a passing remark in the Braden article.

15 This was Edward Moody McCook, 1833-1909. He was, prior to being Governor of the Territory, the U. S. Minister to Hawaii from 1866 to 1869. He was also a Civil War cavalry commander serving with the 2nd Indiana Cavalry, receiving several brevets for gallantry and meritorious service. (Webster's *Biographical Dictioniary.*, p. 938.)

16 This was General James W. Forsyth, a graduate of the United States Military Academy, class of 1851. He served as Aide-de-Camp to General Sheridan, as a Lieutenant Colonel, from 13 March 1869 to 17 March 1873, and then Military Secretary to General Sheridan from 17 March 1873 to 4 April 1878. (Heitman, p. 430.)

17 This is just the opposite of Elizabeth Custer's own observations, for she stated: "I saw symptoms of that deadly stupor which is the sure precursor of freezing . . . [some soldiers] afterwards lost their feet, and some of their fingers had also to be amputated." (Custer, op. cit. p. 22.)

18 For a far more descriptive narrative of this historic moment, all of Chapter II, pp. 17-29 of *Boots And Saddles* should be read.

19 Braden's description hardly approaches the drama of that of Mrs. Custer. But General Godfrey's unpublished account tells a vivid story:

". . . landed at Yankton April 13th, 1873. Early on the morning of the 15th, Braden, myself and others were waiting call to breakfast when we saw a horseman madly approaching, beating his horse with his sombrero. When several hundred yards from us he began yelling 'Get out of here, get out of this as quick as God Almightly'l let you.' As he came up, I recognized Gen. Ed. McCook, Secretary and Acting Governor of Dakota Territory. I said, 'Hello, General, get down from your high horse and tell us what's the matter.' He replied, 'You've got to get out of here as quick as God Almighty'l let you. A blizzard is coming and you've got to take your men and horses to town and get under cover. Every stable, warehouse and public hall is at your service.' 'But, General, tell us about a blizzard.' 'A big storm, you've got to get out of here or you'll be snowed under.' 'But General, we can't move without orders. You'll have to see the C. O., General Custer.' And then we pointed out a partly constructed home just outside the limits of the camp where General and Mrs. Custer were billeted. The sun was shining brightly, it was warm spring, but spread above the western horizon was a dense black cloud and above that were filmy mare's tail clouds that betokened wind. We hurried breakfast and got orders to take men and horses to the town. Afar big drops of rain began to fall just as we started to town three miles away. The wind came with a blast bringing with it snow flurries and rain; the wind became a gale and then of hurricane velocity. The air was filled with ice particles that stung our faces and blinded us so it was with great difficulty we could make progress, none mounted, constantly struggling with the horses which became almost frantic. Near the town a citizen piloted us to a warehouse on the bank of the Missouri where Braden and I put our troops' horses. Then we started for the hotel to find out where we could put our men. After struggling some time against the storm we found ourselves on the bank of the Missouri again. A second start was made and again we came up against the Missouri. Then we made another effort. Placing our backs to the river I made a few steps in advance and halted, Braden directing me to the right or left and then he would come up; in this way we were progressing when we came up to a citizen and asked him if he could pilot us to the hotel. He replied he didn't know whether he could make it but would try. I took hold of his coat tail and Braden took hold of mine. We finally reached the hotel well nigh exhausted. Pilots were sent to conduct the men to a hall where they were billeted. The third day after we were able to get relief parties put to our camp where women and children were imprisoned under fallen timbers. The streets of the town were filled with drifted snow to the tops of the houses, packed like ice by the driving winds. Communications were opened through tunnels over the sidewalks. Fortunately the temperature had not been too low. To this day the event is referred to as *The Great Blizzard*.

"We left, as it were, our 'mark' on the landscape. We had several car loads of Blue-grass-hay from Kentucky, the seed from which, on the campsite and for miles below, wafted by the winds, had fallen on good ground, germinated and eventually supplanted the wild grasses of the valley and is referred to as the *7th Cavalry Blue Grass*." (Godfrey to Roe, pp. 3-6.)

Braden had a wonderful talent for understatement.

[20] This is the Battle of Washita, the Federal View of which can be read in *General Custer and the Battle of the Washita: The Federal View,* for it contains all the important Federal documents and reports of that famous confrontation with the Cheyennes. That book was edited by this editor.

[21] David Sloan Stanley of Ohio who graduated from the United States Military Academy on 1 July 1848, and who first saw service with the 2nd Dragoons. On 28 September 1861, he received the rank of Brigadier General of Volunteers, and on 29 November 1862, he was promoted to Major General of Volunteers. He received several brevets during the Civil War. Though mustered from Volunteer

service on 1 February 1866, he received appointment to Colonel in the 22nd Infantry on 28 July 1866, and eventually Brigadier General in 1884. He retired 1 June 1892 and died on 13 March 1902. (Heitman, p. 915.) He had been a strong and willing leader throughout his military career, but was a heavy drinker, a fact which created many problems for the Northern Pacific Railroad surveyors in the 1872 Expedition, and the major factor which was to lead to the problems with his junior officer, Custer, in the 1873 Expedition. The only real evidence of this turmoil exists only in letters fully revealed in my Foreword; they do not appear in official reports.

22 The expedition's official reports are most difficult to read and interpret from the original today, not only because of the fading, brown ink most commonly used then, but the elaborate scroll confuses the now dim writing. From Stanley's official report we find the following units reported on the expedition:

Ten Companies Seventh U. S. Cavalry; Lieutenant Colonel George A. Custer, 7th Cavalry, Commanding.

Ten Companies Eighth and Ninth Infantry; Lieutenant Colonel L. P. Bradley, Ninth Infantry, Commanding.

Three companies Seventeenth Infantry and one Company Sixth Infantry; Major R. E. A. Crofton, Seventeenth Infantry, Commanding.

Five Companies Twenty-second Infantry; Captain C. J. Dickey, Twenty-second Infantry, Commanding.

Detachment of twenty-seven Indian Scouts; Second Lieutenant D. H. Brush, Seventeenth Infantry, Commanding.

One Company Twenty-second Infantry (E) was organized as pioneers; two Artillery squads, manning two 3-inch Rodman guns, being selected from the same Company.

"As a part of the military force, I was authorized to hire scouts, guides and interpreters, and employed seven half-breeds in that capacity. The transportation, including every wheeled vehicle, amounted to 275 wagons and ambulances. The civilian employees numbered 353 men. the number of mules and horses to be foraged was 2,321." (Stanley, David S., *Memoirs*, pp. 244-45). The companies of the 7th Cavalry on this expedition were A, B, E, F, G, K, L, M. (AGO, *Actions With Indians*, p 55.)

General Stanley's main guide was Basil Clement.

23 This is Second Lieutenant Daniel Harmon Brush of Illinois, who began his military career as a Private in Company F, 145th Illinois Infantry, but later attended the United States Military Academy, graduating on 1 September 1867. He was appointed at once to the 17th Infantry, and was there assigned as commander of the Ree Scouts during the 1873 Expedition. He was to attain the rank of

Yellowstone Expedition of 1874 75

Major before retirement. His father served gallantly during the Civil War and was brevetted Brigadier General of Volunteers for actions at Fort Donelson and Shiloh, Tennessee. They both shared a common name. (Heitman, p. 256.)

[24] Glendive, Montana is located about 75 miles northeast of Miles city, and as such was on the natural path on any march from Fort Lincoln westward.

[25] Frederick William Benteen, Captain, Brevet Colonel, of the 7th U. S. Cavalry, about which more will be said in the volume of the Little Big Horn battle.

[26] James Peleg Kimball of New York and a veteran of the Civil War. But at the time of this expedition he was a surgeon in the U. S. Army. He died April 1902. (Heitman, p. 598.)

[27] Francis Marion Gibson of Pennsylvania who first saw his commission as a Second Lieutenant in the 7th U. S. Cavalry on 5 October 1867. He retired as a Captain on 3 December 1891. (Heitman, p 453.)

[28] Charles Camilus De Rudio, originally from Italy. He received his education in the Austrian Military Academy, and later served on the staff of General Garibaldi in Italy. He then came to this country and enlisted as a Private in Company A, 79th New York Volunteers on 25 August 1864, but was discharged on 17 October 1864, and a month later was commissioned a Second Lieutenant of Colored Troops. He served in the 2nd Infantry until his appointment was cancelled, only to be removed on 25 October 1867. He did not join the 7th U. S. Cavalry until 14 July 1869, and was promoted to First Lieutenant on 15 December 1875, and Captain on 26 August 1896. He died on 1 November 1910 in Los Angeles at the age of 78. (Carroll, John M. and Byron Price, *Roll Call On The Little Big Horn,* p. 125). There is some evidence he may have attempted to Anglicize his name in later years for his death certificate lists his name only as Rudio. There is an excellent article on him in *Army Magazine,* August, 1964, "The Tart-Tongued Bomb Thrower of the Seventh Cavalry." His popularity within the ranks of the 7th Cavalry has always been questioned, and his activities during the Battle of the Little Big Horn have been questioned by many. Charles K. Mills has uncovered some very interesting material on this officer from a book, *Orsini: The Story Of A Conspirator,* by Michael St. John Packe. Apparently there is some impression that Mrs. De Rudio was somewhat successful in passing herself off as some sort of countess. Packe says that she was a "confectioner's assistant" and that *di* Rudio married her "to save her mother's shame." He also states that *di* Rudio was attempting to make a living as a language teacher in England, but wasn't much of a success because he could barely write his own language, Italian. He also states that the *di* Rudios were so wretchedly poor that their neighbors in East London swore afterward that they had never seen such a miserable family. Apparently *di* Rudio was a double agent — a

76   Cavalry Bits

police informer — so other revolutionaries were convinced. One stabbed him six times in a restaurant in Haymarket in April 1856. He was roped into the Orsini conspiracy because one of Orsini's men was literally, financially supporting *di* Rudio's wife. Packe described *di* Rudio as "pathetic." Eliza *di* Rudio was a witness for the Crown in a trial that sent her benefactor, and others, to prison. Providing Packe's sources are correct, this places the *de,* or *di* Rudios squarely in England before coming to America, a fact not generally known.

[29] It is interesting to note here that there was a colored woman who went along on this expedition as a cook. No objections were ever raised about her, indeed no notice ever given, but her name does appear on the rolls. Yet, General Stanley took great pains to object to Custer having a Negro cook with his command. (Stanley, op. cit., Letter from him to Mrs. Stanley, in the Field, 28 June 1873, p. 239.)

[30] This may or may not be true. The Lewis and Clark Expedition had a black servant, York, who, as the stories go, left in his wake scores of children whom he fathered. Just after the Civil War, Isaiah Dorman, escaped slave of the D'Orman family of New Orleans, according to Robert Ege, settled in Montana and took as his wife a Sioux woman of the Uncpapa tribe. There may have been others, cowboys who drifted throughout the land, even prospectors, but the blacks were in the northwest for a very long time — long before the 1873 Expedition.

[31] An excellent description of the Two Bears village and family is written by Mrs. Custer. Her attitudes and impressions were somewhat different — perhaps more diplomatic — than those of Braden. (Custer, Elizabeth, op. cit, Chapter VI, pp. 60-72.)

[32] Brigadier General Alfred Howe Terry of Connecticut. His first commission was as a Colonel in the 2nd Connecticut Volunteers on 7 May 1861. His service capabilities and accomplishments during the Civil War are unquestionable. He was nominated for and confirmed as a Brigadier General, United States Army, on 15 January 1865. He attained the rank of Major General on 3 March 1886, and retired two years later, almost to the day. He died on 16 December 1890, at the age of 63. (Carroll & Price, pp. 158-59.) Although his capabilities were unquestionable, his capabilities in Indian warfare were certainly subject to question. His vagueness in instructions to Custer before the Little Big Horn have been grist for historians and hacks alike for over a hundred years. Though little of the accusation for Custer's defeat was levelled against him — ever — Terry must have felt much guilt and most certainly talked frequently with his brother-in-law, Colonel Robert P. Hughes, who may have felt duty bound to protect Terry's reputation (again, which was not in general question or under criticism), and had published an article in his defense. (Hughes, Robert P., "The Campaign Against The Sioux in 1876," *Journal of the Military Service Institute of the United States,* January 1896). Otherwise,

why the article, and by one who was not there or under attack by any party or parties? This article can also be found as an appendix to Colonel William A. Graham's *The Story of the Little Big Horn, 2nd Edition*, no pagination. It is not included in the 1st Edition.

33 George Walter Yates of New York, who distinguished himself in the Civil War first as an enlisted man with the 4th Michigan Infantry, and later as a Captain in the 13th Missouri Cavalry. He received two brevets during the Civil War. This was one of the officers to die at the Little Big Horn in 1876, and buried at the battlefield, but on 3 August 1877, he was re-interred in the Fort Leavenworth National Cemetery. (Carroll and Price, p. 164.) Correct name as verified by the Yates family was George Wilhelmus Mancius Yates, though he usually signed it "Geo. W. Yates." His mother was Margaret Mancius of Albany. (Letter, Brian Pohanka, 26 Jan., 1982.)

34 This was David A. Lyle from Ohio, who graduated from the United States Military academy on 15 June 1869, and was assigned to the 2nd U. S. Artillery. He was on duty at Fort Wrangel, Alaska, only from 10 May to 27 September 1870. He died on 10 October 1939 at the age of 92. (Heitman, p. 648.)

35 *The Josephine* was put directly into service on the Missouri in 1873 *after* the expedition had begun. Captain Grant Marsh had had the *Josephine* built from his own specifications and for his own use. She originated from the marine ways at Freedom, Pennsylvania, and was considered the newest addition to the Coulson Packet Company at the time. Captain John Todd had gone east for the purpose of hastening its construction and delivery, and when Captain Marsh saw the *Josephine* for the first time, he transferred to her from the *Key West*. She was of very light draught, having been designed to use on the Missouri and Yellowstone Rivers where water depths varied. She was named after General Stanley's little daughter, then at Fort Sully. She was ordered directly to the Yellowstone for government contract service with the army in the field, consequently her first service was to the Yellowstone Expedition of 1873. (Hanson, Joseph Mills, *The Conquest of the Missouri*, pp. 183-184). She was to see much service in the Sioux Campaign of 1876, though not as dramatically as the *Far West*. The *Josephine* had a length of 178', a beam of 31', a hold depth of 4'6" with a net tonnage carrying capacity of 300.51. (Lass, William E., *A History of Steamboating on the Upper Missouri*, p. 108.)

36 Edward Pennington Pearson, 17th U. S. Infantry, who began his career as a Private in Company A, 25th Pennsylvania Infantry in 1861. At the 1873 Expedition he had been in grade for eleven years and was not to be promoted to Major until 1881, eight more years. He did attain the rank of Brigadier General of Volunteers on 30 November 1898, but retired six and a half months later, 16 May 1899. (Heitman, p 779.)

[37] Stanley, in his official report, stated catagorically that Company E, Twenty-second Infantry was utilized as pioneers, yet we have Custer performing that duty as well. And Braden further stated the cavalry troops took turns with this duty. Stanley was negligent in giving credit where it was due.

[38] Custer's favorite scout, as any book will tell you. An excellent biography of this scout has been written by Ben Innis. It was apparently the wife of Dr. Benjamin F. Slaughter who was the first to make contact with Bloody Knife. He appeared at her door one day at Camp Hancock and presented her with a freshly taken scalp boasting all the while it was the scalp of a Sioux. Mrs. Slaughter gave Bloody Knife an order for ten pounds of sugar, apparently his price. Later, Billy Jackson was to relate Custer sent for Bloody Knife that very evening, held council with him about the hostile Sioux and their probable location. Jackson further stated: "Ever after . . . Bloody Knife was Custer's favorite scout. Very quickly, at any rate, Custer and Bloody Knife were 'Sihuan,' Arikara for friend, to one another." (Innis, Ben, *Bloody Knife*, pp. 85-86.)

[39] This was the engagement between Troops A and B, 7th U. S. Cavalry, under command of Myles Moylan, in which the official reports state one enlisted man and one Indian wounded. (AGO, *Actions With Indians*, p. 55). This was also the first major breaking of the famed Laramie Treaty of 1868, one which many ignore, some preferring to place the blame of the "official" breaking of the treaty on the U. S. Army and the 1874 Expedition into the Black Hills. One has only to read the treaty, especially Article II, and specifically sub-paragraphs 1, 2, 3, 4, 5, 6 and 7. (Kappler, Charles J., *Indian Treaties, 1778-1883*, pp. 1001-1002.)

[40] The persons killed were Dr. Holzinger, the veterinarian of the 7th Cavalry, and a Mr. Baliran, a sutler. The spelling of these two men's names vary from account to account. For the purpose of this book, I've spelled them as they appeared, and often slightly different. The soldier killed was Private Ball. Edgar I. Stewart states: "Mrs. Custer states that Dr. Holzinger was shot first and rode a short distance before falling from his horse. Then the Sioux beat out his brains with an iron mallet and filled his body with arrows. Meanwhile, Mr. Balarian had managed to hide in some bushes but was soon discovered by the Indians. He held up his hand as a gesture of peace, and later gave Rain-in-the-Face his hat as a petition for mercy, but it availed him nothing. Neither man was scalped, as Holzinger was bald and Balarian wore his hair close cropped, but both bodies were shot full of arrows and otherwise badly mutilated. (Stewart, Edgar I., *Custer's Luck*, pp. 59-60). Stewart seems to believe Rain-in-the Face was not the responsible party, but was hunting buffalo some hundred miles to the northwest. Nonetheless, it gave rise to the famed feud between Captain Tom Custer and Rain-in-the-Face, the former arresting the latter. Rain-in-the-Face, supposedly swore

revenge, to cut out Tom Custer's heart, and this grisly event has been celebrated in verse, "The Revenge of Rain-in-the-Face," by Henry W. Longfellow, an excerpt reading:

> But the foeman fled in the night,
> And Rain-in-the-Face, in his flight,
> Uplifted high in air
> As a ghastly trophy bore
> The brave heart that beats no more,
> Of the White Chief with yellow hair.

(Dippie, Brian, *Bards of the Little Big Horn*, p. 243). It is at this point things become fuzzy since the feud was with Tom Custer, but Longfellow has the General's heart "uplifted high in air." In any case, the event is fanciful. What is disturbing is the lack of information and reporting on Private Ball. He apparently was not killed at the same time as were Holzinger and Baliran. Nonetheless, he was "surprised at a spring and probably killed before he could make a defense. The bodies of the civilians were found unmutilated; the soldier's remains were only found as we returned in December." (Stanley, p. 250) "Dr. Houzinger (sic) was a corpulent old man, quietest and most inoffensive habits, a great favorite with the regiment." (Whittaker, Frederick, *A Complete Life of General George A. Custer*, p. 471). Baliran presented yet another problem to Custer and Stanley, as related in the Foreword. Benteen had this to say of him: "At Memphis, Tennessee, Balarian was a proprietor of a restaurant and gaming establishment, doing a good business, and a gambler by profession. Having some money, Custer induced him to come with the 7th Cavalry as Sutler telling him the officers of the regiment were high players, and he could make a big thing, 'catch them coming and going.' Balarian told all this to De Rudio on '73 trip and De Rudio told me Custer had put in 0, but had drawn out to that time, $1,000." (Carroll, John M. *The Benteen-Goldin Letters,* pp. 255-56.) Benteen, in his usual promptness to denounce Custer, could have been telling the truth. However, Marguerite Merington reported: ". . . Mr. Balarian, who is a great favorite with our officers asked me what he should do [referring to an order by General Stanley]. I bade him come into camp with me . . . and no one has been hanged as yet." Merington herself wrote: "The Sutler's store was outside the camp proper. Mr. Balarian came, accordingly, as guest of the officers." (Merington, Marguerite, *The Custer Story,* p. 251.) Stanley was also to write of the two men: "The trader leaves a young wife and baby in Memphis. He was one of the men who gave me much worry by disobeying orders and bringing liquor, but I forgive him now, and am sorry for his untimely fate. The Veterinary was a fine old man of sixty, a widower with grown up sons." (Stanley, p. 242.) Too little biographical information exists on Holzinger and Balarian, and far too little thought has been given Private Ball, whose body lay undiscovered for weeks, an unfitting tribute to a brave soldier. The name of the soldier who gave the warning has been lost to history.

41 As mentioned before, Edgar I. Stewart casts doubt as to whether Rain-in-the-Face was even there, much less responsible for the deed. This may be so, but there is no doubt that the boasting of Rain-in-the-Face of having performed the perfidious deeds was the factor which caused his own arrest. Rain-in-the-Face was always facing difficulties in proving himself to the other Sioux leaders and his boasting may have been calculated to increase his prestige. This is pure speculation, of course.

42 Godfrey tells it this way: "On the 8th of August we struck a trail of lodgepoles and General Custer with eight troops of the 7th Cavalry and the Indian Scouts were sent ahead to follow the trail. August 10th we came to what later became known as Pease Bottom where the trail led across the Yellowstone to the south side. Every effort was made that day to cross the river but it was a bank full from a storm in the upper valleys, and the current too swift to be negotiated. Early on the morning of the 11th a solitary Indian was seen to come to the south bank of the river to water his horse. He dismounted to let his pony go down the bank, when he discovered our bivouack, jerked his pony back, mounted and disappeared in the woods. A soldier going to the river for water, nearly opposite, saw the Indian as he pulled the pony back and gave the alarm. (Godfrey to Roe, p. 10). Pease Bottom was not to receive its name until 1875 when Crow Indian Agent Major Fellows D. Pease first built his trading post there.

43 This was Private Michael Keegan who had been born in Wexford, Ireland, and at the time of the Yellowstone Expedition of 1873 was enjoying his fifth enlistment. He was discharged on 15 December 1876, at Fort Abraham Lincoln. There is a record of his death on 23 July 1900. (Hammer, p. 213.)

44 Braden, in characteristic understatement, attempted to minimize his injury. Fortunately, General Godfrey, an eyewitness, recorded the event: "The river had fallen considerably and preparations were being made to cross when a number of shots were fired from the woods on the opposite bank, and soon after the Indians appeared in force. Our scouts reported that the hostiles were seen coming down the valley on the north side. Captain Yates was ordered to send a detachment of 20 men under a lieutenant to cover the flank on the ridge. Lieutenant Larned was Yates' Second Lieutenant, but declined to take detachment because he was Engineer Officer of the expedition, so Braden was detailed for that duty. Braden advanced to the brow of the ridge, but held his fire till the mounted hostiles came close up the opposite slope when both sides opened fire. The hostiles were repulsed but Braden fell. A bullet had shattered his thigh bone. For many years pieces of the bone worked down to the knee and were extracted by the surgeons. This was before the discovery of X-ray. His suffering was indescribable. His immediate suffering was not

only from the wound but in bringing him to camp he was bumped in the cactus beds which abounded in that region and the thorns caused great pain. The surgeons were for amputation, but Braden heroically and emphatically said NO. (Godfrey to Roe, p. 11.)

45 William Hall was born in New York City and enlisted in Troop L, 5th U. S. Cavalry, on 31 October 1865, in Washington, D. C. He was discharged as a Private in that unit on 31 October 1868, at Fort Wallace, Kansas. On 22 March 1869, Hall re-enlisted at Fort Leavenworth, Kansas, in Troop L, 7th U. S. Cavalry. He was discharged as a Private in that unit on 8 May 1874, at Fort Leavenworth. On 25 April 1879. he re-enlisted as a Private in Troop L, 7th U. S. Cavalry, at Fort Abraham Lincoln, North Dakota, and deserted from that post on 24 July 1879. He apparently held the rank of sergeant for a short period of time, but was reduced in rank for some infraction in March 1874. (Letter, National Archives, 24 June 1981.)

46 Thomas Henry French of Maryland. He was to serve Custer and the 7th gallantly, but succumbed to "demon rum" sometime after the Battle of the Little Big Horn. In fact, his drinking habits were to be the cause of his court martial and dismissal from the service. It was a questionable complaint lodged by Mrs. De Rudio whose "sensitivities" had been assaulted when Captain French was supposedly seen drinking and cavorting with a washerwoman in her tent while Captain French had been in command of a movement of troops and civilians from Camp Sturgis, Dakota Territory, to Camp Ruhlen, Dakota Territory, in August, 1878. The drinking was perhaps unquestionable, but his behavior with the washerwoman was doubtful. On 26 March 1879, by General Court Martial No. 19, Headquarters of the Army, Captain French was found guilty of most of the several specifications and dismissed from the service, President R. B. Hayes recommending only suspension from rank on half-pay for one year, this from the Executive Mansion on 22 March 1879. On 5 February 1880, Captain French retired from the service, and by General Court Martial Orders No. 17, Headquarters of the Army, 12 March 1880, the unexecuted portion of the court martial sentence was remitted. (Carroll and Price, p. 129, and Carroll, John M. ed., *The Court Martial of Captain Thomas H. French*, May, 1979). Two years later, on 27 March 1882, Captain French, while living in retirement at Planters House at Fort Leavenworth, Kansas, died and was buried there in the National Cemetery. On 4 March 1891, by family request, his remains were disinterred and sent to Washington, D. C. His remains were reinterred in a family plot at Holy Rood Cemetery which is privately administered by Georgetown University.

47 Thomas Ward Custer, the General's brother, was not a West Point graduate, as was his illustrious sibling. He began his military career as a Private in Company H of the 21st Ohio Infantry on 2 September 1861, but by 8 November 1864, he held the rank of Second

Lieutenant in the 6th Michigan Cavalry. He earned many brevets including First Lieutenant to Lieutenant Colonel, all for distinguished service. He was also the recipient of two Medals of Honor for actions in the Civil War. Like his brother, he lost his life on the banks of the Little Big Horn, but exhumed in July, 1877, and reinterred at Fort Leavenworth National Cemetery, his brother's remains going to the cemetery at West Point. (Carroll & Price, p. 124.)

48 This was really Hiram Henry Ketchum, Braden misspelling his last name. Canadian born, he entered the service of the United States as a Private in Company K of the 16th New York Infantry in 1861. He served in that rank until 23 February 1866, when he received a commission as Second Lieutenant in the 13th Infantry. He transferred to the 22 Infantry in September of that year. He was a First Lieutenant at the time of the 1873 Expedition, and was later to be brevetted a Captain for actions with Indians near the mouth of the Big Horn River on 11 August 1873, the day Braden was wounded. He retired as Major on 11 August 1898, and died the very next day. (Heitman, p. 595.)

49 There is a large hillock standing between the coulee behind the "Pease Bottom" encampment and the camp site. The artillery was run up this mound and fired at the Indians across the river. It is not known how many rounds were fired, but two percussion caps from an artillery piece have been found, one by me and it is now in my private collection.

50 This incident is both humorous and, of course, one of danger at the same time. There were no injuries or loss of lives at that short engagement, but it has been the inspiration for two paintings, one by J. K. Ralston, and the one which appears as a foldout in this book.

51 Patrick Henry Ray was a First Lieutenant in the 8th Infantry at the time of the expedition, but had transferred from the 33rd Infantry in 1867. Again, this was a fine officer whose career began as an enlisted man in 1861, private, corporal, sergeant and first sergeant in Companies K and A of the 2nd Wisconsin Infantry and the 1st Wisconsin Artillery. His commission came in 1863. He eventually attained the rank of Lieutenant Colonel in the 7th Infantry in 1901. (Heitman, pp. 817-18.) Stanley misnamed him Philip Henry Ray (Stanley, p. 241.)

52 Fort Berthold was located in North Dakota. In 1864, troops were sent to protect the trading outpost of Fort Berthold, which was located on the north bank of the Missouri River about thirty miles below the mouth of the Little Missouri River, where the Garrison Reservoir now covers the site. In 1865, a military post was formally established there, but abandoned in 1867. (Prucha, p. 61.) It was, by the time of the expedition, the agency of the Indian Reservation.

53 The identity of this officer is undoubtedly Captain (Brevet Brigadier

General Volunteers, and Brevet Lieutenant Colonel, Regular Army) William Thompson of Pennsylvania and Iowa, who commanded Company B of the 7th U. S. Cavalry. He was on detached service at Fort Rice from June 19 until October 27, 1873, when he went on a 30 days leave. He is mentioned in Libbie Custer's books as a curious and eccentric older officer.

54 The returns of the Yellowstone Expedition of 1873 indicate that only the captain from the 6th U. S. Infantry was on that campaign, Captain James W. Powell, Jr. Captain Powell was from New York, and he began his military career as a Private in Company B, 7th New York State Militia. He eventually rose to the rank of Colonel in the 17th Infantry and retired from the service on 8 September 1899. (Letter, National Archives, 23 October 1981.)

55 Another slight error, but characteristic, was the omission of any sufferings and problems faced by this wounded officer from the day he received his wound until return to his permanent post. Additional descriptions will appear in the next article, but I believe it important now to include General Godfrey's continuing narrative:

"But the expedition, now reunited, must go on. Attempt was made to carry him [Braden] on a hand stretcher, but the hot weather and unbroken trail soon broke the details down; it was humanly impossible. The jolting of the ambulance on the rough rocky trail gave such excruciating pain that his life, at the end of the first day, was almost despaired of. Then it was discovered the Q.M. Col. E. D. Baker, had a buggy stored in one of the wagons. Gen. Stanley ordered that it be dismantled and connected into a stretcher bearer — long poles connected the running gears — a mule for power except in very rough places. The mule was unhitched and the men hauled by hand; a wagon cover served as a canopy to keep out the direct rays of the sun, but the heat and dust were almost unbearable. Lt. Smallwood, Braden's classmate, with his company of Infantry, was assigned as convoy. And so it was up the Yellowstone to Pompey's Pillar, then across the Musselshell River, down the valley to The Big Bend. There the Expedition divided, the 7th Cav. and the Northern Pacific survey making direct route to the Yellowstone at the Glendive under General Custer. The supply train and infantry under General Stanley going direct to the Yellowstone, but that hope was not realized till they got to the Supply Camp at the mouth of the Powder River. There Braden was put aboard the steamer, *Josephine,* and taken to Fort Lincoln, Dakota Territory.

"I did not see Braden again until he rejoined the regiment at Fort Rice, in the spring of 1877, hoping he might be able to do light duty. but the regiment took the field and Braden was granted sick leave until he was retired in 1878.

"When I reported for duty at West Point in '79 Braden was there to welcome me. He was teaching the Post School. He was made

Secretary of the Association of Graduates. In those days the reunions were banquets at the Officers Mess. Visitors complained that they could not get accommodations at the hotel and when I was on the Executive Committee I proposed to Braden that we get the Superintendent to order vacated the Angle rooms and turn them over to visiting graduates That was the beginning of the present accommodations for reunions.

"Braden's sturdy character, his abstemious habits, his devotion to duty, his directness or bruskness gave many the impression that he was uncompanionable, unapproachable, but those who knew him well, knew that he was congenial, companionable, gentle in his feelings, generous and kindly disposed He had no use for cant or subterfuge. He was sympathetic; but if a person played on his sympathy, and Braden later found it was pretense, he never forgot or forgave a breach of confidence." (Godfrey to Roe, pp. 12-13.)

Godfrey's narrative was written at the request of General Roe at the death of Braden. Excerpts and rewritten parts of this narrative were used in Braden's obituary.

An Incident of the Yellowstone Expedition of 1873[1]

anon.[2]

About 8 o'clock in the morning of August 11, 1873, on the north bank of the Yellowstone River in Montana, in a spirited fight between eight troops of the Seventh Cavalry under General George A. Custer and Sioux Indians, Lieutenant Charles Braden, of this regiment, was shot through the upper left thigh. The bullet, from a Henry rifle, fired at a range of not over fifty yards, went clear through the leg, badly shattering the bone and splitting it down to the knee. The Lieutenant was dismounted and walking with his right side towards the Indians. The left leg was in the air when struck and as the wounded man fell, his weight coming on the broken bone, caused the ends to pass each other and stick into the flesh, making a very ugly wound. One of the sergeants with his detachment wore a long black silk scarf.[3] This he took off and tied it as tight as he could around the leg above the wound.

Lieutenant Braden's detachment numbered about twenty men of L Troop, and was in advance guard about a mile ahead of the main command. The detachment met a large number of mounted Indians, but succeeded in holding its position until several troops of the regiment arrived and drove off the Indians, pursuing them some distance up the valley.

Lieutenant, now Commissary General Weston, rode to where Braden lay, unstrapped an extra blanket from his saddle and left four men and a bugler[4] to take charge of the wounded man, ordering them to put him in the blanket and take him to where Custer had established his headquarters. The bugler was to lead the horses and carry the carbines of the four soldiers, who carefully put Braden in the blanket, and each carrying at one corner, started for the field hospital.

It was necessary to go across several large ravines, and up and down hills, The bugler, who became scared, could not manage his extra horses and carry the four carbines, disappeared. This left the party unarmed. Then one of the contract doctors with the expedition appeared and said the Indians were coming back, and the carrying party had better hurry or they would all be killed. This message greatly accelerated the pace, and the party went as rapidly as possible. Some patches of cactus had to be crossed; the prickers were long, dry and brittle.

For a few minutes the men carrying the blanket were able to keep it from touching the ground, but they soon became tired and the injured man frequently hit the cactus. Many of the prickers went through the blanket into the flesh and broke off. It seemed as if every square inch of his anatomy that had come into contact with the cactus had at least a hundred of such broken spears. They afterwards were the cause of much pain and suffering.

After awhile the party reached headquarters. Dr. Ruger,[5] brother of General Ruger,[6] U.S.A., retired, pulled the pieces of bone out of the flesh and made the patient as comfortable as possible. There were no appliances to dress such a wound, and there was nothing to do but wait for the wagon train to arrive, which it did about sundown.

Dr. James P. Kimball, U.S.A., recently deceased, was the chief medical officer of the expedition. There were no splints or plaster bandages in the medical wagon, so the doctors, aided by a blacksmith and a carpenter, having obtained a few pieces of boards by breaking up some boxes used for commissary stores, made a trough long enough to hold the entire leg. The trough, or box, was open at the top;

across the bottom was fastened a tourniquet, which held two strips of adhesive plaster, about three inches wide, fastened one on the inside and the other on the outside of the leg, and extending up to where the bone was broken. On the left side of the box was screwed an iron rod, reaching along the body and bent at the shoulder so as to pass under the neck. Two other strips of adhesive plaster, about the same width as those used below the break, were put on the leg. One of these strips was stuck to the front of the body and the other to the back, and both were fastened to the iron rod under the neck. The object of these strips was to hold the leg in place and keep the ends of the broken bone from rubbing against each other, and to prevent, if possible, shortening of the leg. Before these strips of adhesive plaster were applied, the leg and body were shaved so that a better hold could be had by the plasters. It is unnecessary to say that the pulling in opposite directions of these strips was not one of the pleasant sensations to which humanity is sometimes treated. A cushion of tow and cotton was made for the box, and the leg, prepared as above described, consigned to what many said would be its last little bed.

The work of making the box and setting the injured leg was done after dark. The only light was from candles held by soldiers, and was very poor. The doctors said that the pain of setting the broken bone would probably be intense as no anesthetic could be given because none was on hand.

Two officers, one, Lieutenant, now Colonel Godfrey,[7] the other's name cannot be recalled now, were asked to hold the patient's hands so as to keep his finger nails from being sunk into the flesh.

A majority of the five medical officers present favored amputation. Dr. Kimball told the wounded man the result of their consultation, saying that in either case the chances to survive the long journey ahead would be about equal if the leg was cut off or left on. The patient decided to keep his leg.

It was realized by everyone that the task of carrying such a severely wounded man was going to be serious. The expedition could not be delayed on his account. He, with the other wounded, could not be left behind with a small guard, for the command was not to return by the route it was to go. General Custer proposed that a raft of dry cottonwood logs be built and the wounded man, with two men as escorts, be floated on it down the Yellowstone River to the nearest post, Fort Buford.[8] The distance was about two hundred and fifty miles, and it was calculated that the current would carry the raft about four miles an hour. The floating was to be done by night, and during the day the raft was to be concealed in the bushes. Lieutenant Benjamin H. Hodgson,[9] Seventh Cavalry, a classmate, afterwards killed in the Little Big Horn fight, asked to go along as one of the attendants.

The scheme was not approved by General Stanley, commander of the expedition, for various reasons. One of his characteristic remarks was that it would be more humane to shoot Braden at once rather than have him captured en route by the Indians or have his raft wrecked and he be drowned in the Buffalo Rapids, which were a short distance above the mouth of Powder River.

When the expedition moved out the morning after the fight the wounded officer, with a soldier who had a broken arm, was put in an ambulance. In order to get the benefit of a beaten road the ambulance was to travel after the wagon train. The jolting of the ambulance was simply awful; the soldier with the broken arm got out and walked. After going about ten miles the doctor reported to the commanding officer that Braden was rapidly losing strength and could not last much longer, so the expedition halted and went into camp.

The next day a new plan was tried. It was proposed to carry him on a stretcher. He was put on one, and at first two men carried it. Each pair carried the stretcher till they were tired, when two others relieved them. Progress was slow, fatiguing to the men, and very uncomfortable to the occupant of the stretcher, who had no protection from the broiling sun. After going three or four miles in about five hours, the carriers were exhausted and camp was pitched. It was seen that this plan was a failure and suggestions were in order. The wagon-master proposed to rig up a conveyance and was told to go ahead. He used the running gear of an ambulance, took out the reaches and cut two small cottonwood poles about six inches in diameter and thirty feet long. The ends of the poles were securely fastened to the springs of the ambulance. Four slings, made of rawhide, were attached to the poles. Into these slings were inserted the handles of the stretcher. The slings were of such a length and so placed that the stretcher hung in the middle of the conveyance about eighteen inches about the ground. Wagon bows were fastened to the poles and over these bows was placed a canvas wagon cover to keep off rain and sun. The conveyance looked much like what are sometimes, in the country, called "stone-boats," where a low platform hangs from the body of the wagon.

The wheels of the rig were wrapped with hide. The object of this was to widen the surface so that the vehicle would run more easily. Wide tires would have been a great improvement, but the rawhide wrapping was not a success. It was all right while the hide was soft and pliable, but when it became dry and hard there was an uneven surface to the wheels which caused jolting.

On the underside of the stretcher boards were nailed so that the canvas could not sag. A thin mattress was put on the stretcher and on this the invalid lay. The next morning, when all was ready for the start, the handles of the stretcher were inserted in the slings and Lieutenant Braden was strapped to the stretcher so that he could not fall off. Two mules were hitched on, the driver riding one of them. When the mules started or stopped there was an unpleasant jerk, and the patient would have been thrown off had he not been tied fast. He did not mind the swaying of the stretcher from side to side but the longitudinal motion was unpleasant, for at every stop or start there was a jerk which seemed to make the ends of the broken bone rub together and caused intense pain. After the first day's trip it was seen that the conveyance, with a few changes, would work very well.

Ropes were run from the handles of the stretcher to the opposite axles so as to prevent the longitudinal swing; a stick was nailed across the poles in such a position that Braden could hold on to it. The mules were given up and the wagon was hauled by men. A detail of thirty cavalrymen and three non-commissioned officers was sent, and at Lieutenant Braden's request, Lieutenant Smallwood,[10] Ninth Infantry, a classmate at West Point, was detailed to take charge of the outfit. The detachment was divided into three reliefs of ten men and a corporal or sergeant. The reliefs were changed every hour. Ropes were fastened along both sides of the vehicle and to the tongue. One man walked alongside each wheel; two were at the end of the tongue to guide, and four others pulled at the rope.

The duty of the men at the wheels was to ease them over ruts or stones in the path. The change of motive power from mules to men was a great improvement, for the wagon was started and stopped without any jerking or jolting.

In order to have as good a road as possible, the outfit was made to follow the wagon train. A hospital steward and several attendants accompanied the party. About every half hour he inspected the condition of the patient. The steward was provided with a keg of water and stimulants, and occasionally gave a small quantity of brandy and water. When Braden became weak and exhausted, word to that effect was sent ahead to General Stanley and he always stopped for the day at the next good camping place. At first about one and a half miles an hour could be made under average conditions. One annoyance which could not be avoided, was the dust which was thrown up in quantities by the wheels and covered the stretcher and its occupant.

As the party moved along some wag remarked that the thing resembled the hook and ladder truck of a village fire department.

The command marched faster than the men could drag the conveyance, so the escort was usually from one to several hours late in reaching camp. Braden's tent was always ready upon arrival, and the stretcher was lifted from its place and put on the ground, where it remained till the next day's march began.

The trip, for the first two weeks especially, was a severe and trying ordeal. No one expected Braden to live from day to day. On the eighth day the march was long, hot and dusty. It was nearly dark when his party reached camp. He was so covered with dust that his features could not be distinguished. A number of officers and men were waiting for him.

Dr. Kimball took hold of his wrist and said, "I can't feel a thing. I guess he is dead."

The report spread that Braden had died and preparations were commenced to make a coffin for him out of a wagon box.

After a couple of weeks the ends of the broken bone had begun to knit and mules were again put to the conveyance, but the four men were kept at the wheels till the journey's end.

It was frequently necessary to ford streams. When this happened one of the men would wade across first. If the water did not reach higher than a certain part of his legs, the conveyance would be dragged over, the bottom of the stretcher sometimes just skimming the water. If the water was too deep, the stretcher was taken out and six men carried it over on their shoulders.

Lieutenant Braden was hauled in this conveyance for twenty-eight days and in it traveled about four hundred miles, as measured by the odometer.

The last day's journey was on the 10th of September,

when the reserve camp at Glendive, Montana, was reached. After remaining there some days the sick and wounded were put aboard the steamer *Josephine* for a trip down the Yellowstone and Missouri Rivers. The water in both was so low that the boat spent more time on sandbars than in motion, and it was early in October before Fort Lincoln was reached.

The leg was taken out of the box and the adhesive straps were removed sixty-two days after the fight. It was a long time to be in one position. During the trip, with no proper nourishment, the body became greatly emaciated, and the flesh in several places was worn down to the bone, causing bad sores. To add to the discomfort, the cactus prickers above mentioned caused ugly little ulcers, which festered. The patient could not be turned over, and in order to attend to these sores, he was held up by six strong men, and the doctor, from underneath the raised body, dressed the ulcerations and put on collodion with a camel's hair brush. It felt like hot coals as the liquid touched the raw flesh.

Several incidents, perhaps worth relating, occurred during the long and awful journey. Two soldiers, one a Holland Dutchman named DeGeer,[11] and an Irishman named Keegan,[12] were detailed to attend Braden. Their tent was always adjoining his, and he could distinctly hear their conversation, and is probably one of very few persons who have listened to the details of their own funerals. One night, about the third or fourth day, when he seemed to be weakening rapidly, he heard Keegan say: "Well, when the Lieutenant dies he will have a dacent (sic) funeral. He won't be sewed up in a bag as were Honsinger and Ballaran, (sic) but he is going to have a real coffin made out of a wagon box. It has all been arranged." Honsinger, the veterinary surgeon, and Ballaran a post trader with the expedition, were killed by the Indians on August 4th. Their bodies were recovered before the Indians mutilated them; the redskins had rifled the pockets of the dead men, but were chased away before they could do any scalping. The remains were sewed in canvas and carried one day before being buried. This was done to keep the location of their graves from the Indians, who would undoubtedly have dug up the bodies. They were buried at sundown the night after they were killed. A picket line was put over the burial place and the next morning the entire train passed over it, completely obliterating every sign of a grave.

Keegan and DeGeer were fluent talkers, and their conversation and arguments was the source of much amusement to the wounded officer. The poor, faithful fellows did not attend his "dacent funeral" as they expected to do, but were, it is believed, afterwards killed in the "Custer massacre."[13]

One day an early camp was made near "Pompey's Pillar."[14] Several hundred of the men were in the river and others were washing clothes. Suddenly a small party of Indians, concealed in the bushes across the river, opened fire. The bathers lost no time in getting out of the water. It was a ludicrous sight to see the men, some carrying their clothes, scurrying for camp. Fortunately no one was hit. The Indians quickly mounted their ponies and scampered off before any of our men could shoot at them.

One night Braden's tent was pitched on a patch of dried grass. Early next morning (reveille was at three, breakfast about four, and the advance at five every day) when the striker came into the tent with breakfast, he put his candle on the ground. The candle tipped over and set fire to the grass. The blaze was noticed at once by Braden, who used his lungs to such good advantage that in less than a minute fifty men or more were there. They cut the tent ropes, threw down the tent, and stamped out the fire. It was a narrow escape for the helpless man.

The last day of the eventful journey was on the 10th of September, just thirty days after the fight. The steamboat *Josephine* was in sight, and the end of a tedious journey was within an hour of its close. Suddenly the mules hitched to the conveyance started to run, and ran a mile before they could be stopped. In crossing some patches of cactus, the hoofs had knocked off some dry pieces; a number of these had hit the bellies of the animals and the pain caused stampede. No damage was done, but imagine the feelings of the helpless occupant of the wagon, who expected an upset, or a breakdown, when the promised haven of rest was so near.

Dr. Kimball took personal charge of Lieutenant Braden's case. He was taken from the regiment and kept with the headquarters of the expedition. About ten days before Glendive was reached, on the return trip, the Seventh Cavalry, under Custer, was directed to cut loose from the main column and take a short route to Glendive, through the "Bad Lands." The infantry with the wagon train was to go where it was known they would have a good trail.

An exceedingly pretty and thoughtful incident happened the day Custer separated from the main command. It may best be described by the following extract from a letter written by him to Mrs. Custer, and published in her book entitled *Boots and Saddles:*

* * *

> Our mess continues to be successful. Nearly every day we have something nice to send to Lieutenant Braden. Only think of him with his shattered thigh, having to trail over a rough country for three hundred miles! He is not transported in an ambulance, but a long stretcher arranged on wheels about thirty feet apart, pulled and pushed by men on foot. They carry him much more steadily than would horses or mules. It requires a full company of men each day to transport Mr. Braden in this way. He is with the main command, but was doing well when we left. The day the command divided I had the band take a position near the route where the rest of the expedition would pass, and when he and his escort approached they struck up 'Garryowen.' He acknowledged the attention as well as he could.

The acknowledgment consisted of reaching out under the cover and waving a handkerchief.

All of the officers of the Seventh Cavalry assembled to greet their wounded comrade and wish him a safe and pleasant journey. The day Custer left the main column it turned toward the Yellowstone River. The march continued till after dark. No water was found, so a dry camp had to be made. Only a few tents were pitched and the mules were not unharnessed. Some miscreant stole Braden's water keg. It was a contemptible thing to do under the circumstances, and he would have fared badly, with no water to bathe the inflamed wound, had not a small quantity of this necessary liquid been husbanded by the hospital steward. The thief had he been known, would have been roughly treated by the attendants.

General Custer had taken his cook, a colored woman named Eliza,[15] along. Late at night, the day of the fight, while the doctors were busy dressing the wound Eliza came to the tent. She brought a lemon, saying it was the last one left in the General's mess, and that it would do Mr. Braden more good than any one else. Kindhearted Eliza! It surely was a very thoughtful act on her part.

Afterwards, whenever the cavalry camp was near headquarters, Eliza always made some good nourishing soup and sent it over. Had it not been for her kindness Braden might have starved.

Captain Andrew Burt,[16] Ninth Infantry, now Brigadier General, retired, was with the expedition. He was a great hunter, and whenever he succeeded in getting some game, always sent a generous share to Braden. Another gentleman to whom Braden was indebted for a number of kind acts was a Mr. Barron, correspondent of the New York *Tribune*. Mr. Barron is, it is believed, now a clergyman and editor of a religious journal published in Boston.

Upon arriving at Fort Lincoln Lieutenant Braden was taken to the post hospital, a ramshackle, wooden structure, situated on the high bluff where the infantry post was located. The only ward was occupied by enlisted men, so Braden was taken to the attic where there was no heat. Through holes in the roof the stars could be seen at night and the sky in the daytime. Between the rafters, where they rested on the frame, was an open space. The place was cold, extremely desolate and dreary.

A few days after being put into this attic, a driving snowstorm came up during the night. By morning several inches of snow had drifted in through the openings, and it covered Braden's bed with a shroud like mantle. He was then taken downstairs and his bed placed in the dispensary. There was some warmth there from an old stove, but it was not a pleasant place for an invalid, as it was also the doctor's office, and sick call was held there.

When wounded he weighed about 180 pounds. After being able to hobble on crutches, the commissary scales at Lincoln showed his weight to be only 125.

Could Braden have been taken to a hospital soon after the fight, he might have recovered with quiet and proper care, but the wound completely disabled and unfitted him for further active service. He was subsequently retired as a first lieutenant. The leg became shortened nearly two inches and partially stiff at the knee, but part of the knee stiffness was probably due to an accident at West Point six months before graduation, when a horse fell with him in the riding hall and injured the kneecap. For eight years there were two running sores on the leg, from which, before final healing, thirteen pieces of bone, several chips of lead, and fragments of clothing were taken. An X-ray picture made at West Point some years ago shows that many more pieces of bone never came out, but were caught in the callus that formed around the ends of the broken bone.

Footnotes

1. This article first appeared in *Cavalry Journal* in October 1904.
2. Authorship of this article has eluded us for a long time. Even the recently published index of the magazine from 1888 to 1968 acknowledged no author. However, its author must have been on the expedition; he must also have been an officer. Probably it was a 7th Cavalry officer, but from that point on, it is still a mystery, and why it should be anonymous is puzzling. The style very much resembles that of General Godfrey, but that is no proof of anything.
3. The identity of this sergeant is lost to history, however, he could have been one of five sergeants from that company: First Sergeant James Butler, Sergeant Henry Bender, Sergeant William Cashan, Sergeant Hugo Findeisen, or Sergeant John Mullen (aka James Hughes). The sixth sergeant, Amos B. Warren did not enlist in the 7th U. S. Cavalry until 13 September 1873. (Hammer, Kenneth, *Biographies of the 7th Cavalry*, pp. 206-07).
4. This probably was Trumpeter Frederick Walsh, killed at the Battle of the Little Big Horn in 1876, but was on his first enlistment at the time of the Yellowstone Expedition of 1873. (Hammer, p. 208).
5. Henry Hobert Ruger was born in Niagara County, New York in 1839, and graduated from Jefferson Medical College in Philadelphia. During the Civil War he was assistant surgeon with the 43rd Regiment Wisconsin Infantry and was a contract surgeon with the regular army from 1867 to 1883. (Letter, National Archives, 23 October 1981).
6. General Thomas Howard Ruger of New York. He retired on 2 April 1897. (Heitman, p. 850).
7. This is Edward Settle Godfrey who is referenced so frequently in the previous article. Godfrey began his military career as a Private in Company D, 21st Ohio Infantry, on 26 April 1861, but served in that capacity only until 12 August that same year. He entered the United States Military Academy on 1 July 1863, graduating on 17 June 1867, and was assigned as a Second Lieutenant to the 7th U. S. CAvalry. He was on the Washita Campaign and the Yellowstone and Black Hills

Expeditions with General Custer. He survived the Little Big Horn fight with the Benteen/Reno entrenchment. He was to be awarded the Medal of Honor for distinguished gallantry in action with the Nez Perce Indians at Bear Paw Mountain on 30 September 1877. On 1 April 1932, at Cookstown, New Jersey, he died at the age of 88, and was shortly thereafter buried at Arlington National Cemetery. (Heitman, p. 461). He was a prolific writer and it is his letters and articles upon which many historians rely for life in Custer's Cavalry.

8 Fort Buford was established in North Dakota on 13 June 1866, on the left bank of the Missouri River near the mouth of the Yellowstone, as part of a plan for a chain of military posts between Fort Leavenworth and the Columbia River. The post played an active part in settling Indian troubles and in establishing the Indians upon reservations. It was occupied continuously until its abandonment in 1895. (Prucha, p. 63).

9 Benjamin Hubert Hodgson was born, and is buried in Philadelphia. A cadet at the United States Military Academy, he graduated 15 June 1870, and was immediately assigned to the 7th U. S. Cavalry as a Second Lieutenant. He was killed in the Battle of the Little Big Horn. (Heitman, p. 534). His death was a little bit more dramatic than that. He was shot from his horse while attempting to re-ford the Little Big Horn River in Reno's infamous retreat. Being only wounded, he grasped the stirrup and the leg of a trooper who attempted to then drag him out of the river and than upwards to safety. Upon clearing the river he was once again a prime target; he was shot and killed by an Indian. There is a marker where he fell. He is often referred to as the regimental favorite, obviously being very popular with the officers and the enlisted men. It is reported that Clinton H. Tebbetts, a classmate of Hodgson's, held a seance in 1877, with the dead Lieutenant. In this extraordinary communication Mr. Tebbetts asked if Custer's command had gone into his last fight willingly or not. Hodgson's reply was: "We of course went in willingly for we never deemed defeat possible. We were anxious for a combat with the red devils, and we had it too, but their numbers were too much for us, and we died gallantly . . ." (Carroll, John M., "Word From beyond," *By Valor And Arms Magazine*, October 1974). If only historical research were that easy!

10 Jenifer Hanson Smallwood of Florida. He was a cadet at the United States Military Academy from 17 October 1865 to 15 June 1869, when he was graduated and assigned as a Second Lieutenant to the 2nd U. S. Cavalry. On 17 March 1873, he transferred to the 9th U. S. Infantry where he was at the time of the expedition. He resigned later that year, in December. (Heitman, p. 892).

11 Abraham De Geer was born in The Hague, Holland, and at the age of 25 enlisted in the U. S. Army at Chicago on 28 May 1870. While serving as a Private in Troop L, 7th U. S. Cavalry, he contracted

hepatitis and was discharged for disability on 4 September 1874, at Fort Abraham Lincoln. Before joining the army he had been a clerk. (Letter, National archives, 24 October 1981).

[12] See Footnote #43 in previous article.

[13] Neither one died at the Little Big Horn. De Geer was no longer in the 7th U. S. Cavalry at the time of the fight, and Keegan was on detached service at the Yellowstone Depot at the time, and thereby missed the battle.

[14] Pompey's Pillar is a popular tourist attraction located 28 miles east of Billings, Montana, on Interstate 94. It is privately owned and this large stone outcropping with a natural bluff overlooking the Yellowstone River is registered as a National Historic Landmark. It is there one can see Captain William Clark's signature etched into the stone, the only real physical evidence of the Lewis & Clark Expedition in the northwest.

[15] The author of this article is in error. Eliza had long since left the Custer's and gotten married.

[16] This is Andrew Sheridan Burt of Ohio. He began his military career as first a Private and then a Sergeant in the 6th Ohio Infantry, beginning 20 April 1861. By 14 May 1861, he had been promoted to rank of First Lieutenant, and made rapid rises in rank culminating with the rank of Brigadier General. He retired from the service on 15 April 1902. (Heitman, p. 267).

Afterword

By Dr. Lawrence A. Frost

The importance of the 1873 Yellowstone Expedition cannot be overemphasized. Leaving Fort Rice as it did in the latter part of June, it was able to complete its survey before the full impact of the Panic of 1873 paralyzed the nation. Its completion before the rigors of winter immobilized it was not because of Colonel Stanley's capacity as the commandant of the escort. If anything Colonel Stanley was a deterrent to smoothness of operation; his frequent inebriation delayed rapid advancement along the proposed route thereby adding considerably to the cost of the expedition by his failure to keep the costly steamboats in constant use.

He raved about Lieutenant Colonel Custer's alleged delay each morning because of the time it took to pack a small cookstove yet he held up progress for over a week because he himself was too drunk to give out orders required for the movement of his command. It was only after members of his staff conned him, while he was intoxicated, into issuing an order to destroy the very whiskey he was consuming that he sobered up sufficiently to reassume command.

The sober Stanley was a likeable person; when in his cups he was an incompetent liability in hostile Indian country.

When General Phil Sheridan made plans for exploring the Black Hills the following year (1874) it was not Stanley he selected to organize and command the expedition. Had Stanley evidenced any capacity to fill the position, he surely would have been designated. It was no surprise when it was announced that Custer would assume command.

This survey of the Northern Pacific Railway appears to be the most important national event occurring during 1873. A similar effort had been made in 1872, having originated on the Pacific coast. Though it was heavily escorted by troops under command of Colonel Stanley, the strong resistance of the Indians forced its termination at Pompey's Pillar.

Stanley's instability as a leader, and his tendency to rely upon liquor for support when confronted with responsibility, were reasons enough for not appointing him to head the important Black Hills mission of 1874. Stanley, like General Hancock during his Indian campaign in 1867, had remained in the rear of his troops awaiting word from the point of Custer's cavalry column if he sighted hostile Indians. Custer had orders to make no movement unless he had permission to do so. Hampered by the ineffective tactics of an armchair general in 1867, Custer saw history repeat itself in 1873 with the added gall of having a commandant who loved his liquor.

Custer had seen the supply steamer needlessly detained because of Stanley's continuous intoxication and resultant inability to function properly as the commanding officer. The result was a senseless detention of the supply steamer for a ten-day period at a cost to the Government of $500 a day.[1] The Northern Pacific Railway's chief engineer, Thomas Rosser, considered it a disgrace to the service. It made Custer, a teetotaller, champ at the bit. Yet he retained no resentment on that occasion nor later when Stanley, in a state of intoxication, had him arrested for assuming command in his stead.[2]

Several days later, the sober Stanley repeatedly apologized to Custer. Custer really liked Stanley and said of him that he was "one of the kindest, most agreeable and considerate officers," he had ever served under.[3]

In spite of personal problems, Indian confrontations and logistics, the expedition was considered a complete success, it being reported that "every object for which it was inaugurated having been effectually accomplished. An area of 20,000 square miles of unknown country to the south and west of the Yellowstone has been explored, the Indians thoroughly whipped, and the survey of the Northern Pacific Railway completed."[4]

The remarks just quoted reflect a concensus just prior to Jay Cooke's fiasco. What appears to be a misstatement or an exaggeration was the reference to "Indians thoroughly whipped." A statement of this kind in the semi-official military publication, the *Army And Navy Journal,* should have displayed more honesty. There were competent, reliable military observers with the expedition who could have provided accurate information about the Indians, and their degree of defeat.

Though a sizeable war party confronted the expeditionary force near Pompey's Pillar on August 11, it represented but a fraction of the Sioux nation. Having been driven from the field unceremoniously had taken away their incentive to interfere further with the survey. It was their philosophy to leave the battlefield, when losing, until their "medicine" was right. A return engagement could come when conditions were more favorable for them. Those with previous Indian experience, who rode with Custer and marched with Stanley, knew that it would be just a matter of time before the Indians would display their displeasure over the white occupation of their hunting grounds.

The stage was being set for that anticipated action. These nomads of the Plains were totally dependent upon the buffalo. Indian leaders were intelligent and informed. Many of them foresaw and predicted the destructive influence of the white man. They resolved to do everything in their power to retain the Indian way of life. Custer's Indian scouts had warned him of this many times. The construction of a rail line through the Sioux hunting grounds along the Yellowstone would surely stir them into action. This he understood for he knew the depth of their roots. They held a feeling for land few whites ever had. And there was nothing he could do about it.

Verbally defending Indians was not popular with most civilians nor was it with some of the army brass in Washington. If one wished to progress as a soldier, orders had to be obeyed. With conflict inevitable, it would be well to be as prepared as possible. Needed was a well-equipped, mobile army, larger than the 25,000 men who were spread thinly around the country. The new railroad would take care of the rapid movement of troops and supplies along the Yellowstone but it, with the settlers it would draw, would drive the buffalo herds to the south forcing the Indians to follow. They would be compelled to occupy the area just west of the Black Hills.

The Sioux religious sanctuary known as the Black Hills was the lone portion of this country that remained unexplored. It appeared to have areas within it that would provide fine locations on which to place forts where troops would be readily available in times of Indian hostility. But first, the Black Hills would have to be explored. The Treaty of 1868 seemed to forbid such a move. Generals Sherman and Terry could help decide. They had helped draft the Treaty's provisions; they would know.

This was not a matter that could be delayed. It would be timely to organize a plan that would appeal to the decision makers in Washington. One of the considerations would be that of cost since the need for the expedition had become obvious.

Once Custer had arrived at the newly constructed Fort Abraham Lincoln and had accosted and subdued the numerous problems the new post offered he began presenting suggestions to both Generals Sheridan and Terry as to the feasibility of such a project. Good marksman that he was, he fired each shot carefully. He thought they should explore and map the Black Hills, determine the degree of hostility of the Sioux while doing so, and then arrive at a proper location for the establishment of a fort within the area, in that order. The cost could be determined easily enough, and then balanced against the worth of the enterprise.[5]

Custer had one shot he kept till last, a shot he would use after all of the others had scored. It was the answer to what many would assume to be a costly expedition. He had seen Stanley waste governmental appropriations by bringing the steamboats to a useless and costly standstill while he indulged in a ten-day drunk on the Yellowstone that summer. There would be no boats on this expedition and there would be no Stanley, for the top brass had had enough of him.

That left the target clear for this final shot. He, Custer, knew how to save — yes, make money for the Government. It was a matter of logic and arithmetic. By estimating the amount of hay and grain required for 600 horses and 600 mules, and its cost to the Government, he calculated that the savings by grazing the animals along the route of the reconnaissance would be over $19,000 during their sixty days in the field. No one seemed to have considered this aspect before.[6]

Custer arrived at this conclusion in the fall of 1873 as a result of his experience accompanying Stanley that summer. He advised Sheridan "that the proposed reconnaissance can be made and result in an actual savings to the government."[7]

Sheridan had decided that a large military post in the Black Hills would serve as a threat in the very heart of the Indian country, to the villages of the Indians that raided the settlements.

General Terry at first thought it inappropriate to explore

the Black Hills but concluded later that the Government had a right to enter that portion of the Sioux reservation.

The exploration of the Black Hills was a matter of great concern to the Sioux. Some think it was a direct cause of Custer's confrontation on the Little Big Horn two years later. It was not, though in all probability it accelerated a timetable that was to end in the subjugation of the hostile Indians.

The construction of the Northern Pacific Railway was a necessary accessory in the development of an empire. There were calculated risks Washington felt compelled to take. The nation was in a turmoil as a result of the Panic of 1873. Unemployment was extremely high. The promise of low-priced land in the West, the rumors of gold discoveries, the general feeling of discontent that prevailed, and the Government's desire to bridge and settle a cultivated empire by an assertion of Manifest Destiny were factors that governed the decision to complete the construction of the Northern Pacific Railway.

Monroe, Michigan

Footnotes

[1] Marguerite Merington, *The Custer Story*, p. 260.

[2] Ibid, p. 265

[3] Ibid.

[4] *Army And Navy Journal* (September 27, 1873).

[5] Lawrence A. Frost, *With Custer In '74*, p. 103n.

[6] Ibid, pp. 92-93.

[7] Ibid, p. xv, n. #12.

Appendix

William R. Pywell

William R. Pywell was born on 9 June 1843, in Baltimore, Maryland, a twin to Jane E. Pywell Howlett. He was the son of Robert Redish (the son carries the same initial but not the same name) Pywell, who was born in Barnswell, Northhamptonshire, England on 26 December 1813, and Ann Maria Diggs Pywell, who was born in Baltimore on 17 October 1821. The father died in Washington, D. C. on 20 June 1883 and the mother died at College Park, Maryland, on 26 September 1906. Both were buried in the Rock Creek Cemetery in Washington, D. C.

Early on in his career, 1862-1865, the son was an apprentice photographer, along with Alexander Gardner, under the famed Civil War photographer, Matthew Brady. In 1864, he worked for a while as an independent photographer with his work from that period identified at Big Black River Station and Vicksburg, Mississippi. In 1865, he once again worked with Alexander Gardner with one picture of his identified as the Old Capitol Prison in Washington, D. C.

From 1867 through 1868, he was listed in the Houston, Texas City Directory as "Artist with C. N. Bean." During this same period he practiced his trade in Austin with another pioneer photographer, W. J. Oliphant.

On 9 June 1869, he married a Margaret Schofield in

Washington, D. C. and to this marriage was reportedly born a son, Denzil, and a daughter, Pauline. Pauline married a man named Davidson from Shreveport, and took up residence there.

In 1873, William Pywell was the official photographer of record of the famed Yellowstone Expedition. His oath of office for this experience reads as follows:

"City and County of St. Louis
"State of Missouri   (no date)
"I, William R. Pywell, of Washington City in the County of Washington, District of Columbia, do solemnly swear that I have never borne arms against the United States since I have been a citizen thereof; That I have voluntarily given no aid, countenance, counsel or encouragement to persons engaged in armed hostility thereto, that I have neither sought nor accepted nor attempted to exercise the functions of any office whatever under any authority or pretended government, authority power, or constitution within the United States hostile or inimical thereto; And I do further swear to the best of my knowledge and ability I will support and defend the constitution of the United States against all enemies foreign and domestic that I will bear true faith and allegiance to the same, that I take this obligation freely, without any mental reservation, or purpose of evasion, and that I will well and faithfully discharge the duties of this office in which I am about to enter, So help me God.
"William R. Pywell"

On 7 August 1887, at Bunkie, Louisiana, after a short illness, this pioneer photographer died at the age of 44 years and 2 months, and a note from a family genealogist states he was buried in Shreveport, and if true, it was likely done at the request and direction of his daughter, Pauline.

For over 100 years most of the photographs of this

expedition were "lost" until recently discovered mis-filed under the Whistler Expedition of 1871. It might be noted here that the photographer stated he had destroyed all his glass plate negatives, according to a Mr. Duryee in a memorandum dated 4 April 1877, except the one captioned "Third Camp on the Musselshell." His anger was directed at the government for they failed to buy his photographs as he presumed they would after hiring on as the official photographer. Continued advertisements in the Bismarck *Tribune* obviously failed to sell enough of them to make the maintenance of the plates profitable, hence the statement that they had been destroyed. This was obviously an empty threat, for the glass plate negatives were the ones discovered by the National Archives, but unfortunately they were unidentified.

The only picture to have been known to survive was the one of Custer and the elk he had killed, and it is not included in this series because of its long familiarity. The only other one known by title, also not in this series, is "Indian burial in cottonwood tree." That accounts for 78 known pictures with 12 yet to surface, and that is something that may occur eventually, as I personally believe nothing is lost forever.

For proper legends to these pictures I turned to one of the great scholars on the subject of the Yellowstone Expedition of 1873, John Popovich of Billings, Montana. His reply to me was one which indicated thought and study, and I quote: "I have put the prints of the pictures in numerical order (The pictures are numbered according to the Pywell sequence of numbers which indicate the period and possible time when they were taken, thereby making it possible to give some order to them. -ed.) and find they pretty well follow the time sequence of the expedition as to location. We must remember that Pywell did not get his photographic equipment until about the 15th of July, as I remember, since the equipment came up the river by steamer. Therefore, no pictures could have been taken prior to that date. Another factor must be considered and that is his equipment was so cumbersome and so much time was needed for sensitizing plates, etc., that it would be very difficult for him to take any pictures while routinely on the move. The most convenient time would be during the few rest stops that were made. These could be as follows: July 20-24 during the time the steamer was crossing the expedition over the Yellowstone near the Stockade; July 30th on the Yellowstone above the mouth of the Powder River; August 14th, 15th and 16th at Pompey's Pillar; August 24th on the Mussellshell 15½ miles above the big bend; and August 26th when they only moved two miles to get better grazing for the stock. With that thinking in mind (and with the photographer's sequence of numbers on his plates) I have categorized the pictures to somewhat fit those time frames." John then mused why Pywell hadn't taken pictures of the river crossings by the steamer, or of the great activity which must have taken place there. Some, if he did, must be represented by those pictures which have not yet surfaced. The categories so identified were:

    Pictures 1 to 9 would be in the area of Glendive Creek and the Stockade.

    Pictures 11, 12, and 14 somewhere in the area of the Bad Lands detour and coming down Custer Creek.

    Pictures 16 to 33 from above the mouth of Powder River to above the mouth of the Big Horn River.

    Pictures 36 to 57 in the vicinity of Pompey's Pillar.

    Pictures 58 to 65 overland along Baker's Trail out of Hoskin's Basin.

    Pictures 66 to 97 along the Mussellshell.

    Picture 98, 99 and 100 on the return from the big bend of the Mussellshell.

All photographs carry the numbers and the identification by John along with the legends and other information wherever possible. There are voids between #1 and #100, so the missing 12 could appear throughout the series.

The pictures will carry only the number, but for proper identification at the National Archives #1 should properly read 106-YX-1, and the prefix to each number is the same throughout.

I personally believe the time schedules and time frames as applied, and the known movements plus the photographer's own numerical sequence make for logical references. There is obviously room for error, but difficult to prove.

The return of these pictures — one of the few sets ever known to have been taken of any major expedition - are a true contribution to the pictorial history of the 7th U.S. Cavalry, and though some photographs may appear to be meaningless, it is important to note that many will find relative value to them. At least this many are now preserved for all time. One has to wonder why Pywell took some of the pictures that seem to have no significance. They may have been taken for Professor J. A. Allen or some of the other members of the scientific group.

All photographs in Appendix are courtesy the National Archives.

Photo portrait of William Pywell who photographed much of the Yellowstone Expedition of 1873. From the National Archives.

1 — Area of Glendive Creek and Stockade on Yellowstone River. Notice picketed horses.

2 — Area of Glendive Creek and Stockade on Yellowstone River. May be Hungry Joe Hills near Glendive.

3 — *Possibly the Glendive Creek area near the Yellowstone River Stockade. May be Hungry Joe Hills near Glendive.*

4 — *Area of Glendive Creek and the Stockade on Yellowstone River.*

5 — Glendive Creek area possibly near the Yellowstone Stockade. Notice lone figure at river bank.

6 — Glendive Creek area near Yellowstone Stockade. Camp on extreme upper left of picture is on south side of Glendive Creek and possibly where the stockade existed. Also the site of the river crossings by steamer.

7 — *Area of Glendive Creek near Yellowstone River Stockade.*

8 — *Near the Yellowstone River Stockade in the Glendive Creek area.*

9 — *Glendive Creek area near Stockade on Yellowstone River.*

11 — *General view of the Bad Lands near mouth of Powder River. Notice horses picketed lower right.*

12 — Another view of Bad Lands near mouth of Powder River with picketed horses better shown.

14 — Possibly somewhere in the area of the Bad Lands detour and coming down Custer Creek. Notice again the picketed horses.

16 — From above the mouth of Powder River to above the mouth of the Big Horn River.

17 — From above the mouth of Powder River to above the mouth of the Big Horn River.

18 — From above the mouth of Powder River to above the mouth of the Big Horn River.

19 — From above the mouth of Powder River to above the mouth of the Big Horn River.

21 — From above the mouth of Powder River to above the mouth of the Big Horn River.

24 — From above the mouth of Powder River to above the mouth of the Big Horn River.

25 — *From above the mouth of Powder River to above the mouth of the Big Horn River. Great camp in background could have been the camp of August 7th, 8th, or 9th, all of which were made on bends of rivers.*

26 — *From above the mouth of Powder River to above the mouth of the Big Horn River.*

27 — From above the mouth of Powder River to above the mouth of the Big Horn River.

29 — From above the mouth of Powder River to above the mouth of the Big Horn River.

28 — From above the mouth of Powder River to above the mouth of the Big Horn River. Notice horses picketed near camp tents. There is a strong possibility these are the cottonwood trees between which Honzinger and Baliran were buried.

30 — From above the mouth of Powder River to above the mouth of the Big Horn River.

32 — From above the mouth of Powder River to above the mouth of the Big Horn River. Possibly Castle Rock in background where Lt. Bradley carved his name in 1876.

33 — From above the mouth of Powder River to above the mouth of the Big Horn River. Again, possibly Castle Rock.

36 — Pompey's Pillar.

38 — In the vicinity of Pompey's Pillar.

39 — In the vicinity of Pompey's Pillar.

37 — *In the vicinity of Pompey's Pillar.*

40 — *In the vicinity of Pompey's Pillar.*

41 — *In the vicinity of Pompey's Pillar.*

43 — *In the vicinity of Pompey's Pillar.*

44 — *In the vicinity of Pompey's Pillar.*

46 — *In the vicinity of Pompey's Pillar.*

47 — *Encampment near the vicinity of Pompey's Pillar.*

50 — Near Pompey's Pillar.

51 — In the vicinity of Pompey's Pillar.

52 — *Spectacular view of Pompey's Pillar at bend of Yellowstone River.*

54 — *In the vicinity of Pompey's Pillar, possibly on Yellowstone River near mouth of Big Horn River.*

53 — *Photographer's cart and photographer or his assistant atop hill in the vicinity of Pompey's Pillar.*

55 — *Area in the vicinity of Pompey's Pillar.*

58 — *Overland along Baker's Trail out of Hoskin's Basin.*

56 — *Yellowstone River opposite Pompey's Pillar. Unidentified person sitting on Pompey's Pillar, possibly the photgrapher or his assistant. This picture appears in Lt. Braden's account.*

57 — *Photographer's cart in vicinity of Pompey's Pillar.*

63 — *Overland along Baker's Trail.*

61 — *Encampment along Baker's Trail.*

61 — *Photographer's cart and possibly traveling over Baker's Trail. Figure believed to be Fr. Valentine Sommereisen.*

59 — *Overland along Baker's Trail.*

64 — *Overland along Baker's Trail.*

65 — *Spectacular view of movement of wagon train overland along Baker's Trail.*

66 — *Along the Mussellshell River, probably at the crossing of August 19th.*

67 — *Along the Mussellshell River. Notice soldier in mid-stream bathing.*

68 — *Along the Mussellshell River.*

74 — *Along the Mussellshell River.*

69 — *A buffalo kill near the Mussellshell River.*

70 — *Camp near the Mussellshell River.*

72 — *Wagons stopped along the Mussellshell River.*

76 — *Along the Mussellshell River. Notice soldiers either bathing or washing clothes in river.*

77 — *Along the Mussellshell River.*

79 — *Along the Mussellshell River.*

80 — Along the Mussellshell River.

88 — Along the Mussellshell River. Camp in background could be "Third Camp on the Mussellshell" near present city of Roundup.

82 — *Bloody Knife posing for photographer. Notice studded rifle butt.*

83 — *Bloody Knife. Notice combination of uniform of Indian dress.*

84 — Stunning photograph of Bloody Knife. Notice saddle, prairie belt and stripes on coat.

85 — *William Pywell, the photographer, taken either by assistant or soldier or even Bloody Knife.*

86 — Custer's "King of the Forest" probably taken in front of his tent, around 24th of August. Possibly near the present-day city of Mussellshell, Montana.

The only William Pywell photograph believed to have survived until those in the Appendix were discovered in 1982. They represented a "lost" colection for over 100 years. This picture does compliment the picture of presumably the same elk pictured in front of what is believed Custer's Tent in the appendix collection. From the Custer Battlefield Collection.

90 — Along the Mussellshell River.

91 — Inland along the Mussellshell River.

93 — *Bear kill, but by whom unknown. Near Mussellshell River.*

95 — *Along the Mussellshell River. Notice soldiers bathing along its banks.*

96 — *Soldiers bathing on banks of Mussellshell as well as in mid-stream.*

97 — *Along the Mussellshell River.*

98 — *Along the return from the big bend of the Mussellshell River.*

99 — *On the return from the Mussellshell. Excellent view of camp and picketed horses.*

100 — On return from the Mussellshell. Spectacular view of horses probably on a picket line or rope.

INDEX

Arnold, Major Abraham K., 11
Augur, Jacob A., 13

Baliran, Auguste, 28, 29, 30, 37, 78, 79, 92
Ball, Private John H., 78, 79
Barnitz, Capt. Albert, 28, 29, 38
Barron, Mr., 95
Battle of Cold Harbor, 12
Battle of the Little Big Horn, 10, 12, 13, 81, 82, 88, 93, 97, 98, 99, 106
Battle of Milk River, 12
Battle of the Rosebud, 12
Battle of the Washita, 46, 73
Battle of Wounded Knee, 10
Bell, Gen. J. Franklin, 13
Bell, William G., 24
Benteen, Capt. Frederick W., 13, 30, 31, 32, 36, 38, 47, 75
Bismarck, N. D., 43, 44
Black Hills Expedition, 25, 36, 102
Bliss, Gen. Tasker, 15
Bloody Knife, 52, 78
Braden, Lt. Charles, 43, 67, 71, 72, 73, 78, 80, 82, 83, 84, 85, 86, 88, 90, 91, 92, 93, 94, 95, 96
Bradford, Gen. Karl S., 13
Brown, Lt. W. C., 12
Brush, Lt. Daniel, 47, 74
Burt, Capt. Andrew A., 95, 99

Cairo, Illinois, 43, 44, 69
Calhoun, Lt. Fred, 31, 32, 33, 39
Calhoun, Mrs. James, 44, 47, 71
Carr, Camillo C. C., 13
Carter, Gen. William H., 13
Chaffee, Gen. Adna R., 13
Chaffee, Adna R. Jr., 19
Combat Forces Journal, 22
Cook, Jay, 103
Cooke, Gen. Philip St. George, 10
Craig, Gen. Malin, 13
Crittenberger, Willis C., 19
Crook, Gen. George, 10, 12
Crosby, Gen. Herbert, 13
Custer, Elizabeth, 30, 34, 44, 46, 47, 71, 72, 94

Custer, Lt. Col. George A., 10, 25, 26, 27, 28, 29, 30, 31, 32, 33, 34, 35, 36, 37, 40, 45, 51, 52, 54, 55, 56, 58, 59, 61, 76, 78, 79, 80, 83, 85, 86, 88, 93, 94, 95, 98, 99, 101, 102, 103, 104, 105, 106
Custer, Capt. Tom, 61, 78, 79, 81

DeGeer, Pvt. Abraham, 92, 93, 98, 99
DeRudio, Lt. Charles C., 47, 75
Dorman, Isaiah, 76

Edgerly, Capt. Winfield S., 13
Eighth U.S. Infantry, 47, 63, 82
Eisenhower, Gen. Dwight D., 19
Eliza, 95, 99
Eltinge, Maj. LeRoy, 18

Forsyth, Gen. James W., 45, 72
Fort Abraham Lincoln, 26, 44, 50, 53, 65, 69, 80, 92, 95, 96, 99, 104
Fort Berthold, 64, 82
Fort Buford, 88, 98
Fort Knox, 23, 24
Fort Leavenworth, 9, 10, 11, 23, 81, 82
Fort Reno, 10
Fort Rice, 28, 29, 31, 44, 46, 47, 49, 65, 70, 83, 101
Fourth U.S. Cavalry, 11
French, Capt. Thomas, 61, 81
Frost, Dr. Lawrence A., 101
Fuller, Capt. Ezra B., 13, 17

"Garryowen", 61, 94
Geronimo, 10, 12
Gibson, Lt. Francis M., 47, 75
Glendive, Montana, 47, 49, 50, 51, 75, 92, 94
Godfrey, Capt. Edward S., 13, 70-71, 72-73, 80, 83, 84, 87, 97
Goldin, Theodore, 26, 38
Grant, Col. Fred D., 29, 30
Graw, Gen. Robert W., 19

Haines, Gen. Oliver L., 13
Hall, Sgt. William, 60, 81

Hancock, Gen. Winfield S., 33, 102
Harbord, Capt. James G., 15
Hardie, Capt. Francis H., 15
Harney, Gen. William S., 10
Harper's Weekly, 15
Haycock, Ernest, 12
Hazen, Gen. William B., 36
Henry, Col. Guy V., 12, 13
Henry, Guy V. Jr., 12
Herr, Gen. John K., 13, 20
Hodgson, Lt. Benjamin H., 88, 98
Holbrook, Gen. Willard, 13
Honsinger, Dr. John, 53, 56, 78, 79, 92

Indian Territory, 10
Infantry Journal, 21

Jackson, Billy, 78
Jackson Barracks, La., 43, 68
Jacobs, Gen. Fenton S., 13
Josephine, 51, 77, 83, 92, 93
Journal of the U.S Cavalry Association, 9-24

Kecheson & Reeves, 11
Keegan, Pvt. Michael, 59, 80, 92, 93, 99
Ketchum, Hiram H., 29, 82
Keyes, Gen. Geoffrey, 22
Kilburn, Gen. Charles S., 13
Kimball, Dr. James P., 47, 48, 75, 86, 91, 94
King, Gen. Charles, 12
Kromer, Gen. Leon, 13

Lannen, Sgt. John, 15
Lee, Gen. Fitzhugh, 10, 15
Lyle, Lt. David A., 77

MacArthur, Gen. Arthur, 15
MacArthur, Gen. Douglas, 13, 24
McCook, Gen. Edward M., 45, 72
Marsh, Capt. Grant, 77
Marshall, Gen. George, 13
Memphis, Tenn., 44
Merritt, Gen. Wesley, 13, 14, 15
Missouri River, 43, 44, 47, 50, 92
Moylan, Capt. Myles, 12, 55, 78
Muddy River, 28

New Orleans, La., 43

New York *Tribune*, 95
Ninth U.S. Infrantry, 47, 90, 95
Northern Pacific R.R., 25, 31, 43, 102, 103, 106

"Old Bill", 16, 17

Paddock, Lt. J. V. S., 12
Parker, James, 13
Patton, Gen. George S. Jr., 17
Pearson, Capt. Edward P., 51, 77
Pease Bottom, 80, 82
Pershing, Gen. John J., 13, 17, 18
Pompey's Pillar, 61, 83, 93, 99, 102, 103
Powder River, 51, 88
Powell, Capt. James W., 83

Rain-in-the-Face, 54, 78, 80
Ray, Patrick Henry, 29, 31, 32, 34, 63, 82
Remington, Frederic, 15, 16
Reno, Maj. Marcus, 12
Rhodes, Gen. Charles D., 13
Richardson, Gen. Robert C. Jr., 13, 17
Rockenbach, Gen. Samuel D., 17
Roemer, Jean, 10
Ropes, John Codman, 10
Rose, Gen. Maurice, 19
Rosser, Thomas, 25, 26, 30, 31, 102
Ruger, Henry H., 86, 97
Ruger, Gen. Thomas H., 86, 97

St. Paul, Minn., 44
"Samuella", 47, 48, 76
Seventeenth U.S Infantry, 47, 51, 83
Seventh U.S. Cavalry, 12, 29, 30, 32, 33, 34, 36, 43, 68, 74, 80, 83, 85, 88, 94, 99
Sheepeater War, 12
Sheridan, Capt. Michael V., 43, 69
Sheridan, Gen. Phil, 45, 102, 105
Sherman, Gen. William T., 10, 11, 104
Sixth U.S. Cavalry, 11, 47
Sixth U.S. Infantry, 65, 83
Slaughter, Dr. & Mrs. Benjamin F., 78
Smallwood, Lt. Jenifer H., 90, 98
Smith, Lt. Algernon E., 34
Stanley, Gen. David S., 25, 26, 27, 28,

29, 30, 31, 32, 33, 34, 35, 36, 38,
47, 49, 51, 56, 61, 73, 74, 76, 78,
79, 83, 88, 90, 101, 102, 103, 105
Stilwell, Gen. Joseph W., 19

Terry, Gen. Alfred, 26, 49, 76, 104, 105
Third U.S. Cavalry, 15
Thompson, Capt. William, 83
Tongue River, 52
Truscott, Gen. Lucien K., 19
Twenty-Second U.S. Infantry, 47, 61
Two Bears Family, 49, 76
Turning, Major, 44, 69

Upton, Emory, 11
U.S. Cavalry Association, 9-24

Voorhis, Daniel V., 19

Wagner, Col. Arthur L., 15
Wainwright, Gen. Jonathan M., 19

Wallace, Edward S., 20
Wallace, Lt. George D., 30, 31, 39
Wallace, Lew, 10
Walsh, Trumpeter Frederick, 97
West Point, 10, 50
Weston, Gen. John F., 43, 45, 47, 53, 55, 57, 59, 69, 85
Wheeler, Gen. Joseph, 10
White, I. D., 19
Wilson, Gen. J. H., 15
Wint, Capt. Theodore J., 11
Wood, Gen. Leonard, 15
Worth, Major, 26

Yankton, S. D., 44, 46, 47, 70
Yates, Capt. George W., 50, 60, 77, 80
Yellowstone River, 47, 51, 55, 57, 80, 85, 92, 95, 104, 105
York, 76
Young, Gen. Samuel B. M., 13

Zogbaum, Rufus F., 12